The Galápagos Islands
Evolution's Lessons for
Cities of the Future

RICHARD REGISTER

DEDICATION

To all those trying to *build* the ideas in this book.

Table of Contents

Introduction

What do the Galápagos Islands and evolution have to do with the future of cities?

Everything.

The universe is everything, its changes through time called evolution. Evolution in its full sense is, then, everything through time. Can we learn something from evolution itself to make humanity's cities healthy instead of damaging to nature? Could cities actually build soils, help reverse human caused global heating, protect the continuity and normal evolution of our fellow planetary travelers and distant genetic brothers and sisters who are everywhere around us, the plants and animals? We've begun to learn from ecology, which is evolution seen in shorter time spans – decades and centuries rather than millions of millennia into the billions of years – about the importance of biodiversity and conservation of nature, recycling, renewable energy systems. We've saved the whales and developed in many places a strong preference for bicycles and transit over automobiles, and so on.

But what to learn from the larger panorama of evolution? The largest panorama, actually, and its lessons for the largest creations of humanity: our built environments of cities, towns and villages. They are so big we have to get this right.

Our story begins in high drama. It's 1535 in the New World and the Holy Roman Emperor Charles V of Spain has ordered the new Bishop of Panama, Tomás de Berlanga, to Peru with creaky planks and ropes and sweaty sailors: Settle the dispute between its conquistador Francisco Pizarro and another commander, Diego de Almagro. These are dangerous people, unpredictable, not your everyday in-the-street folk. It's said they are dividing Spanish South America into two hostile camps, armies to be more precise. Also, reliable reports of torture, enslavement and wholesale murder of the Inca people have reached Spain, along with enormous shipments of their stolen gold. But the fighting between the conquistadors has to end, the violence against the people must be minimized. The Spaniards' religion, after all, is based on the teachings of the Prince of Peace. Good luck with those well-armed contradictions Tomás!

On the way to Peru the winds fail. Sails hang flat from their yardarms, reflecting in the mirrored undulating Pacific while a relentless current carries de Berlanga and his crew 600 miles out into an unforgiving sea, without a drop of rain, under a burning equatorial sky, bizarrely cold water running all the way along South America from the Antarctic, then turning west, headed straight for Asia 10,500 miles beyond the horizon. If penguins could make it all the way from the calving glaciers of our southern-most continent, maybe de Berlanga is in for some interesting surprises.

What he finds is a volcanic landscape pushing up through the waters in domes and cones of harsh black lava patched over with dry thorn bushes and two-story cactuses scattered everywhere, and believe it or not, with the cold waters, penguins *have* appeared exactly at the equator among the amazing, strange animals with no fear that have never before been seen by humans. The birds there are so tame they land on your shoulders and the giant tortoises look at worst a bit irritated if you sit on their backs. The islands, writes de Berlanga, "…are full of very big stones, so much so that it seems as though at some time God hath showered stones" – and writes off the Islands as unworthy of even a name, which must be close to unique in history for a discoverer of new territory. For the next 300 years these are mostly known as the Enchanted Isles, enchanted in a sense more cursed than beckoning. Back in Europe, thirty-nine years after Berlanga sights these crusty lava islands, and 10,000 miles away, Flemish cartographer Abraham Ortelius, hearing of the impressive giant tortoises in a place he will never see, decides to give the islands their Spanish name for tortoise.

But 300 years later, a blessing these islands are to a young Charles Darwin, who later calls them the cradle of his theory of evolution. The story is written in the differences he records between the animals that appear to be related and yet substantially different from each other from one island to another and what seems like related species in South America. The plants also offer up the same puzzle. "What's going on here?" he asks himself, a question to define the rest of his life and change the history of science and humanity's understanding of "the origin of species," including our own.

But Father Tomás and his crew, on their way to mission impossible, are dying of thirst: water, water everywhere but at 3.5% salt, enough to poison anyone. On the Enchanted Isles they are reduced to sipping crushed prickly pear juice. Two men die of thirst and ten horses. When a breeze finally comes up, they make it back to the continent in terrible shape. Vast areas of the former Incan Empire have been portioned out in two great territories. The competing leaders of the Spanish invasion continue sparring and persist in their brutal governance as before. One must think de Berlanga depressed. Back in Panama he resigns being Bishop within two years – at about the same time Pizzaro corners and "executes" de Almagro.

1

"The Galápagos!
Why didn't I think of that before?"

You and I may see marine iguanas as strange, "imps of darkness" Charles Darwin called them, black, sometimes splotchy gray to match the ragged costal rocks, with serrated spikes on head, neck and back like small dinosaurs. They are the only reptile to swim in water and live on seaweed.

300 years after Bishop Tomás de Berlanga arrives, Charles Darwin visits the Galápagos Islands on a British Navy ship, the Beagle, charting South American coastline waters and the Galápagos Islands. Why all the renderings of the Beagle I can find show the ship in placid waters I have no idea. Said Charles Darwin in his immediately best seller at publishing, The Voyage of the Beagle, *"...weather beaten Cape Horn... demanded his tribute, and before night sent us a gale of wind directly in our teeth. We stood out to sea... and saw on our weather-bow the notorious promontory in its proper form – veiled in mist, and its dim outline surrounded by a storm of wind and water. Great black clouds were rolling across the heavens and squalls of rain with hail swept by us with extreme violence." That Darwin was almost constantly sea sick aboard is testament to his dedication and remarkable perseverance.*

Their bones and cartilage actually shrink making them "grow" smaller as a means of cutting back demand for food in the starvation years of El Niño. Flaming red-orange Sally lightfoot crabs with sky blue leg joints skip about the black cinders sprayed by foaming breakers. They pick among slippery remains of broken seaweed. Cormorants have ratty, shrunken, moth-eaten wings now useless for flying, but not so bad for swimming. Then there are the batfish, red-lipped – just like nice sensuous human lips with red hot lipstick. They are truly strange; look them up! They scuttle, crawl and bunce under the surf along the islands' sloping rocks and sandy bottoms. And the blue footed boobies turn into plunging javelins by the hundreds entering the waters like an invasion from outer space, one dangerous looking smooth splash after another or many at the same time… More like zip-and-bubble than the crash-and-spray of the big pelicans. The boobies' super streamlined forms slice deep into the water *under* the fish, which they catch on their way back up to the surface.

Sally lightfoot crab, upper left; marine iguana under water, upper right; lava lizard with red face – middle left; the famous giant tortoises, middle right; a volcano erupting, lower left; and the landscape of volcanic craters at sea level, lower right.

All that is something you'd think I'd naturally remember when coming to visit Ecuador since I've always been fascinated by the Galápagos Islands wildlife, the Galápagos being a province of Ecuador. But it hadn't occurred to me. I was busy thinking about talking ecological city design to civic leaders in Quito, teachers, students, and the "general public" in televisionland because...

...Rosalia Arteaga Serrano had invited me to give three college lectures, do a television show with her and provide a breakfast talk to about 20 of her friends and associates. She kept me busy and happy. The small old-fashion mansion headquarters of her FIDAL Foundation was perched in the dramatically steep hills of a stylish neighborhood in the capital city, stunning snow-capped mountains all around seven thousand feet higher than any mountain in the contiguous USA. Her mission: largely education for young people and largely about environmental issues.

But it wasn't until an agriculturalist in the small audience spoke after me about his experimental work on the Galápagos Islands that I said to myself, "Why didn't I think of this earlier? The Galápagos would be *the* best place in

3

all the world to connect the way us humans design and develop cities, towns and villages to the lessons to be learned from evolution. It's an utterly amazing place. It's number one on the evolution lover's Earth-exploring bucket list."

These islands are unique on the planet, a window to the deep past we all come from with hints galore about how to proceed into an ecologically healthy future. For the last fifty years or so, society around the world has come to understand a great deal about ecology, despite the counter current into sprawling low-density automobile dependent development. Despite, or perhaps as a reaction against the rapid growth of "sprawl" and automobile dependence over that half century, there are also people in large numbers waking up to the virtues of public transportation and bicycles and beginning to see cars and the spreading suburbs as a highly problematic form of human settlement, driving both agriculture and natural species off the land – *literally* driving them off. That's you and I at 70 mph on the freeways, 15 mph in school zones, zero mph in traffic jams, if that can be "driving." And it all requires millions of acres paved over in parking lots, driveways and garages.

In the Galápagos we could in addition to learning from ecology, begin to learn from evolution as well. One lesson is that evolution is essentially creativity in action, but creation paired with destruction: you have to be careful what you create! By the time you get to conscious creatures in evolution's history, there are choices to be intelligently made, and with consulting conscience too. Specific to the Galápagos there are the many lessons about how species are preserved and even reintroduced as far as possible, in many cases to reverse damage already done.

Lesson number one from evolution for cities, towns and villages now thoroughly dependent upon cars and spread over vast landscapes is this: that complex living organisms are arranged in three-dimensional form, not flat like a sheet of paper. When it comes to cities, towns and villages, also complex in their functioning like living organisms, the scattered two-dimensional from has enormously destructive impacts. It started in the United States soon after the Second World War and now is an urban arrangement dominating life in cities in practically every country in the world. Not the city in general, but this particular form of the city is the culprit. It consumes vast areas of land, paves over nature and farm alike, requires profligate use of transportation energy, loading the atmosphere with greenhouse gasses and probably amounts to the largest single cause of climate change – for just one of its more noteworthy harms.

Low density urban development ranks high among causes of extinction of species too, by simple displacement, driving native plants and animals off the land, as urban sprawl sprawls out. Once the dependence upon cars becomes epidemic even the more-dense parts of cities have become car dependent with as much as a quarter of new buildings' sheltered volume typically stuffed with parking spaces for cars that pulse in and out and about cities in a daily tide of metal, plastic, glass, rubber and commuters consuming whole lakes worth of fuel or powerplants output of electricity.

Again, for emphasis, this is the lesson: that evolution arranges complex living organisms in three-dimensional form, not flat like a sheet of paper. Cities, in so many ways are also complex living phenomena and so we should take the hint: Their swarming cars and vast sprawling suburbs – flat out and gigantic, in simplest terms, two-dimensional – aren't such a good idea.

From the forming of stars in the early universe from scattered hydrogen and helium, to the birth of planets made of the heavier elements cooked up in the larger stars that explode in supernovas seeding space with the building materials of planets, through the planets with their internal looping convection currents of hot fluid stone, grinding plates and pulsing volcanos, to the organizing of living organisms like our own selves on at least one planet, meaning our physical bodies on Earth... in all those steps, evolution teaches us the extreme efficiencies of the well-ordered three-dimensional form and warns us of the inefficiencies to the point of serious dysfunction of... flatness. In fact, flatness is not the format of any complex living entity. This is a powerful and extraordinarily basic lesson for further healthy evolution. Complex higher things and functions simply do not form in the shape of a sheet of paper. They are 3-D. More sculptural than painterly. When it comes to urban layout and design, construction and operation, car/sprawl development works directly against that most basic pattern in the universe organizing itself, evolving: 3-D works for happy evolution, or at least normal evolution as we are coming to know it.

Said young architect philosopher Paolo Soleri back in 1965, "It's not just that cities are in bad shape, it's that they are also the *wrong* shape." He meant not three-dimensional, giving deference to evolution's modeling, but due to adopting cars and sprawl development, two-dimensional.

Is this something worth paying attention to? I certainly think it is. The very creativity of evolution itself is born of the amazing efficiencies of compact, three-dimensional form well organized. For understanding cities, towns and villages I think of this as "the anatomy analogy": cities *like* complex living organisms. And the best place to broadcast the news is very likely from the place best known everywhere as the laboratory classroom called the Galápagos Islands – thank you Charles Darwin.

Evolution is simply the totality, the approaching-infinitely-complex universe, largely getting more so – more complex and intricately, elegantly organized in our times – through us humans in our thinking and acting together... and against each other too. Evolution through time is the largest context of our very existence, all of us, and we, to say the very least, have a noteworthy role in its process being the emergence of consciousness, and, hopefully, conscience in our corner of our galaxy, on our home planet Earth.

Put more than a very small number of people together and we have a collective awareness and product that is cultural consciousness and conscience, the conscience part being us trying to do and teach good works and weave laws for justice, avoid disasters and keep this evolution going.

And what is the largest of human creations? Cities, and with their smaller cousins – towns and villages – the built home of our collective societies. Some folks live isolated out on the range and a few meditate in caves but probably considerably fewer than ten percent of us by now. How should we be designing, building and living in our constructed habitations? In the answer is much of our salvation – if we are to save ourselves and most of the rest of the biosphere in a time of climate change and broad and increasing species extinctions brought on by none other than ourselves.

Above, three-dimensional steps in evolution: 1.) upper left, stars forming out of hydrogen in the early universe, 2.) planets from the debris of exploded stars. 3.) Then living organisms appear, including us humans, 4.) and lower right, the more three-dimensional city, or at least a small town-sized version of the built community in the work of architect Ken Yeang of Malaysia. None are two-dimensional like suburbia.

And where did Darwin get those ideas, anyway? The key ones he said, and recorded to history? On the Galápagos Islands. And where did science take great strides in learning how to preserve and restore endangered species? Well, practically everywhere, but with special emphasis on restoring whole habitats along with particular species right there, again, on the Galápagos Islands. That has happened mainly and specifically through work at the Charles Darwin Research Station, Puerto Ayora, Santa Cruz Island, Galápagos Province, Ecuador.

To me it was crystal clear, simple as basic mathematics:

Evolution's lessons	E
City design (if modeled on the efficiencies of living organisms)	C
Power of the Galápagos to communicate world-wide	P
A very major world solution	S

E x C x P = S

I use x for multiplying rather than + for adding because I believe each of these variables multiplies the total effect of the combination, not just adds up to a modest product but multiplies way up, to resulting in enormous forces at play, if well thought out, to amazing benefit for all life and even seemingly inanimate phenomenon like the temperature of the planet, the state of the climate, the level of the ocean and direction and force of its currents.

Therefore, in following through strictly logically, I had to get to those enchanted isles and see if I could encourage and perhaps actually instigate the building of an ecocity model project, undoubtedly of modest scale, but large enough to influence villages, towns and even cities everywhere. The project could coast into world consciousness on the coattails of the righteously famous if controversial Mr. Darwin and his research so important for humanity's understanding of – no kidding – everything though forever, since that's what evolution is all about.

Could this understanding transform the city-building enterprise of our species from an interesting and culturally productive activity for most of us, but also a colossally destructive process for the environment? Could this understanding metamorphose into activities building far healthier cities, perhaps even ones to contribute not just to a less damaged future but one becoming healthier in the normal pattern of our universe evolving?

Above, setting sails for the model of the Beagle, with the statue of Charles Darwin, hand extended to greet all passers-by. This is in the town of Puerto Baquerizo Moreno, San Cristóbal Island, the Galapagos on a spot very near where Darwin first set foot on the Galápagos Islands.

We can find out and my confidence is that we can succeed. And that depends on if we define the project in some similar way to what I present here and if we try. What excellent timing too that only a few short years ago no less than Pope Francis himself, the Pope from South America, declared the Church now believes in the theory of evolution and sees the scientific "Big Bang" origin of the universe as true and compatible with Catholic beliefs. His reasoning is simple enough: if God created everything, that has to include evolution itself.

I gotta get there! So, I've been to the Galápagos Islands twice in the last two years, thinking through how to create a model project to introduce the world to the ecocity way of building and living – or at least try my very best.

2

What sort of model for the Enchanted Isles

Why get excited about building a small-scale model project, as any project on these modest sized islands with their small populations would indicate? And why would a project, say, on the scale of a small neighborhood down to only one or two blocks, or even a half block, be relevant to larger cities back on the continents? Good questions but also with good answers.

Why early visitors to the islands were discouraged. In the left photo: what can grow was a thorny barrier, and in the right photo we can see why de Berlanga thought God must have showered stones, and why it's hard to keep rain and fog drip from disappearing downwards. Where's the soil? Barely exists. How to build on broken rock? Not easy.

Complete projects, not just finished and built, but complete in the sense of having the essential features and functions present and functioning, seem to be elusive. We are used to, by now, seeing a fair number of "green" buildings with energy conservation and passive solar orientation to sun or shade for comfort and interior "climate control." We have, if rare, solar greenhouses attached to the sunny side of houses delivering warmth in cold weather and at the same time for growing garden starts for transplanting outside the greenhouses. I bought a house with five others in Berkeley, California once and we added a tall attached solar greenhouse on the south. Inside the greenhouse grew two tomato plants reaching all the way to the one-and-a-half-story high ceiling. They produced almost all the tomatoes in our salads for two years, harvested by ladder. Many houses and even apartments have composting going on, some businesses have good materials recycling arrangements. Some families have organic gardens producing food on adjacent enriched soil using household compost. Some use coffee grounds from Starbucks to enrich compost and garden soils at home. I do, frequently bringing home a ten-pound sack of spent grounds for fluffing up the garden soil. Some buildings have a home office or mixed uses such as residential living and arts and crafts production under a single roof, cutting commuting from a matter of miles and hours to feet and seconds – like walking from one side of a good-sized room to the other rather than driving across town. We're learning from ecology.

There are also especially imaginative urban housing developments such as Village Homes in Davis, California that must be one of the best green suburban designs in the world, with narrow, minimal width streets for cars and back yards looking out on a second set of trails for people on foot and for bicycles moving at reasonably faster than walking speeds. Tool and drool along this path system with its fruit festooned trees, corn, grapes, artichokes, baby greens, beans, peas, melons, arms-length and short stepladder accessed nut trees, and the big mulberry that stains everything that juicy pungent bright red. Along these paths it's a sociable second front yard, houses there typically two stories and practically none ever for sale people are so content to live there. Village Homes must be among the most thorough-going food-producing suburban community-style developments anywhere. And, though not car-free, Village Homes is notably car-lite.

Autofreie Stadt (Car-free City), which impressed me on a visit in the mid 1990s, is a project of 244 apartment units in Vienna with a very small number of project-owned cars available for borrowing for special purposes – sign up to drive which most residents do very rarely. If I remember correctly it was twelve adults per each car, getting close to acceptable! Given the presence of frequent and convenient transit service, the richly cultural environment of the ancient city of Vienna is quickly and conveniently available with almost no need, or possibly say *excuse*, for a car.

What about the three-dimensional project I'm advocating in this short book for the Galápagos with its message that the ecocity way of building and living would be supremely healthy? It would also be an easily replicable way of enormously improving the health of living in cities, towns and villages everywhere. On the Galápagos Islands where small scale would be appropriate, the "organic 3-D model" at four or five stories would be sufficient for communicating up-scale, we might say, important lessons to town and city sized communities.

I've seen up to six story buildings in small Turkish villages, Nepalese towns and in Brazilian favelas. There are presently five story buildings already there in Puerto Ayora, with social spaces with views over town, beyond the mildly bustling Academy Bay, over the waves to nearby Santa Fe Island and then to the endless ocean horizon from a few sun-sheltered sixth floor roofs.

And where do we find all those features together? In my history traveling to and giving talks in 36 countries around the world and 30 US states looking, I have never found a genuinely complete "piece of an ecocity," the elusive model for the whole real deal. I've been looking for something to lead us on to a remodel of cities designed around the human body's speed, size and mind, not the car body's and the minimally conscious idea of automobility powered by immense use of fuel, machines, asphalt, concrete and land. Something, or usually some *things*, always seem to be missing. Always completeness counts in nature – but isn't there in the cultural product.

For comparison, how would an herbivore on the Serengeti fare missing one leg? How about a hawk with one eye, thus without the acuity and depth perception of parallax vision, manage approaching a prey that would be dodging predation, and so on? This incompleteness would be a serious handicap in the drama of survival and the said incomplete animal would be considerably less likely to survive to reproduce than a complete one. With ecocity completeness missing, is human evolution handicapped in this way?

That analogy probably isn't totally apt, but what I'm suggesting is that the impressive healthiness of the full-on ecocity would be, as they say, greater than the sum of its parts. It would be a real synergistic arrangement to change things for the far better. Thus, the notion to make a standard example, a self-conscious model to encourage broad replication of "complete" ecocity projects of smallest scale large enough to in fact be complete in the essential features of full-community facilities and functions. Such would be a very important contribution to a much healthier future.

We lack such well-developed "whole systems" designs in the ecocity mode, and yet they are not exotic in building materials or detailing. They don't defy physics, engineering or chemistry. Plus, they are in tune with biology. They are not cities floating above fantastic landscapes from science

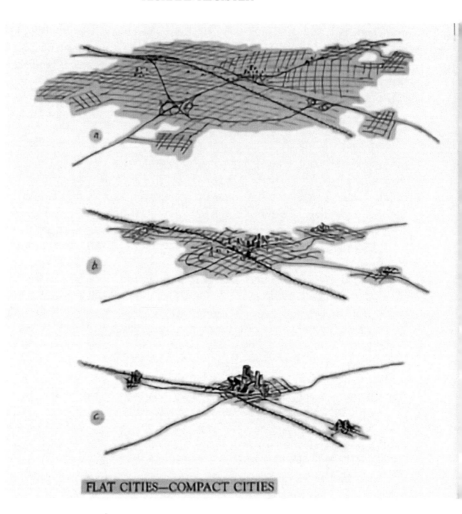

FLAT CITIES—COMPACT CITIES

The above is about as graphically simple as we can get illustrating the difference between sprawl and more three-dimensional compact urban and small-town layouts. The top example (a.) requires radically more land for development and massively more energy for operating than layout (c.). That's because (a.) is thoroughly dependent on automobile infrastructure and the car's demands for land, energy and vast expanses of concrete and asphalt. The two more 3-D versions (all three versions for the same population) represent a greatly reduced physical footprint for the number of people served. Thus, the ecological footprint goes from enormous in the top layout, to reasonable enough for an eco-renaissance in city building in the realms of (b.) and (c.).

fiction book covers, suspended in air by anti-gravity machines. Nobody "beams up" (or down) anybody, or hits "warp speed." Conventional construction materials and methods are just fine. The parts simply need to be pulled together if we are to have a clear view of what they will look like, and if we are to see them in full potential performance. They are not that difficult to draw, either. My book *Ecocities Illustrated* features 206 drawings doing just that: illustrating a profound alternative way of building, all of it easily and conventionally buildable – if we decide to do that.

The style doesn't matter either. Pretty much any style from Victorian to space age modern, adobe Santa Fe style to quirky personal, Bauhaus to your house, will do. But if the functions of community living are in full variety, each function close to the others it should relate to, all's well that continues well.

And what are those basic functions that can be facilitated beautifully by ecocity small projects? There is lodging both permanent and brief: housing and hotels. There is education, some production work in arts and crafts or science, space for office work, professional and business office jobs, food availability in stores and growing nearby. Restaurants needed and cafes, along with basic hardware and pharmacy and so on as the minimum in the traditional village general store, plus maybe the flea market and farmers market. Then there's recreation, especially in a place like the Galápagos, with its educational dimensions, reinforcing what everyone is coming to understand, that thorough recycling of materials, conservation of energy, &c. (as Darwin used to write for etc.) is enormously important. Sports facilities adjacent as people like them. Churches, synagogues, temples and so on, or more generally, places for focused appreciation for our very existence, which could be a walk in the nearby woods or the worship of thunderheads and rainbows from a terrace with a view, holding hands with someone you love.

The most needed of all in our list is getting the layout right and what is often called by planners, the "massing" of buildings, along with the pattern of streets – primarily pedestrian – and open spaces like plazas and parks.

The technologies that make sense are harmoniously integrated into the architecture and arrangement of community functions too. Utilization of solar and/or wind technology – that part of the solution is becoming obvious these days. With the more-dense, intimate, personable village arrangement, whether in town like a neighborhood center, or in the stand-alone village, conservation of land and resources are largely by-products of compact layout and development – with natural landscapes or agriculture immediately outside.

In this arrangement we have facilities and functions in their right places and relationships to other facilities and functions and even resources like incoming solar energy gathered to warm interiors or to generate electricity, or water coming down from the sky to be collected off roofs and channeled into cisterns, for storage underground or stored in tanks on rooftops. Water is then later delivered under gravity's pressure to be used for our many purposes. Wine cellars, and even mushroom growing is appropriate in basements, worm composting under the kitchen sink. In basement or attic simple storage makes sense in trunks and boxes full of meaningful memorabilia, books, Interesting magazines, ancient toys – everyone's different, if similar.

Temperature-adjusting greenhouses should be facing or sheltered from the sun depending on geographic and climate location. Indirect natural "studio lighting" serves for reading, writing, drawing, painting, lots of fabricating tasks. Model making and sculpture makes sense on the shady side of structures for providing even lighting. For both tourists and relaxing locals, the sociable best locations are on street level close to sidewalks for people-watching and with best more distant views, sometimes called "prospect," from terraces and rooftops, &c.

With a little density and small scale but relatively tall structures, the "profile" or "skyline" of the ecocity project needs to be conspicuously three-dimensional enough to read as modestly tall, definitely 3-D. The "look" as well as function, the education as well as primary experience, needs such

Marine iguanas are approachable up to about two feet, and look amazingly lazy when relaxing, even devil-may-care sloppy. Above left, this one was in one position for about fifteen minutes as a lite drizzle fell, then flipped its position just before I took the photo, leaving a kind of rain shadow in the dust. Right, the people and famous approachable island "wildlife" looking far from wild, or some special brand of wild.

features as rooftop paths and bridges connecting buildings on terrace levels knitting the functions of the built ecocity project together in a unified whole. That's the "anatomy analogy" mentioned earlier: cities, villages, even neighborhoods *like* complex living organisms, a serious step in evolution, evolution being appropriate to the Galápagos Islands of course.

Then there is the relationship to the natural landscape and farming outside: in ecocity arrangement that's right out the door, without the fraying out of suburban scattered low-density sprawl in the way... just walk "out" and into such environments in a few steps to a few minutes and you'd be in a whole other non-urban experience. Pedal out and down a path and you'd be in the wild in more like seconds – a minute will get you a long way on a bicycle. When you begin to think bicycle, and consider pedaling at about three times waking speed, that extends your reach to the variety of community offerings nine times over walking in the same period of time. That's amazing transportation power, and powered by just breakfast, lunch or dinner.

With the pieces all in their right places and the whole complete, then we would have a very powerful example for reordering cities, towns and villages around the basics of healthy physical communities. How much potentially more powerful that model would be broadcast out from the Galápagos as instruction for urban design directly from the lessons of evolution as well as ecology? Enormously enhanced I should think. The whole story of Mr. Darwin and the panorama of evolution would come traipsing along with the narrative.

As an activist in the early days of the environmental group Greenpeace has said, Paul Spong by name, "Change can happen at the speed of thought." Linked at the speed of light by electronic broadcast and conversation, with cell phones and computers connected everywhere, that span is not just fast but everywhere on the whole Earth *now*. That also is exactly the sort of thinking that struck me as potential in bringing evolution, city design and the Galápagos together as a means to accelerate "Change can happen at the speed of thought," to not just stunningly quickly but everywhere on the planet at the same time. *If* people tune in to the same wave length – which is exactly what holidays are all about. Holidays?! Hold that thought. We'll get back to it soon.

But back to the physical model that might be built, what's usually been missing that's of first importance in my own international exploration of cities, towns and even villages looking for the elusive complete example? First the three-dimensionally mentioned above, because even the tall buildings are very seldom horizontally connected above ground level. It's more like the towers are extensions vertically of the flat surface, not genuinely 3-D. Simplistically stated, there are very few bridges connecting buildings above ground level, much less, whole networks for movement at a few levels above ground level. The community collective structure is more like a vertically enhanced two-dimensional structure, the street level, if augmented by subways one level down. Some cities, if rarely, have an underground pedestrian path network, such as Montreal Canada's "Underground City," which was almost forced underground by the intensely cold winters there. It is as if people never simply thought about it directly. They were forced by nature there to think about it.

With our model ecocity initiative for the Galápagos, the clear appearance and actual functioning in three-dimensions becomes possible at as few as three or four stories where at terrace level bridges could connect publicly accessible open spaces. Some such spaces would actually be small plazas surrounded by shops, cafés or restaurants, crafts work spaces, hotel lobby entrances, office reception desks and so on. Such plazas can look out over the surroundings with another two or a few more stories rising up from this already elevated public space defining what I call "keyhole plazas."

The name comes from the plan of the plaza looking down at it from above, the plaza itself looking something like the keyhole in old fashion locks with a slot for the notched key flange extending out and down from the hole. In the keyhole plaza, that slot is the direction of the view out from the plaza between enclosing buildings to outside landscapes, seascapes and other locally appreciated views. There are some such elevated mini-plazas spaces in some larger hotels, but those are often missing some other features and functions in close proximity and usually don't utilize passive solar warming or shade from the layout and design of the buildings for cooling. Or the ensemble is not plugged into the best of recycling or only occasionally on an edge with a notable view, or lacks bicycle facilities and connectivity, and so on.

Why not for such elevated prospects, exterior glass elevators for the sheer entertaining inspiration of watching the landscape fall away or rise up as you move up or down, from one roof, terrace or ground level location to another level? The vertical motion itself is education/promotion for ecocities helping make movement through the "infrastructure" a pleasure in itself. Ditto for walking or biking from one part of the overall structure of buildings to another over elevated bridges, a touch of adventure in your town.

Then there is the "lost in the urban" experience, best exemplified by the narrow public and commercial pedestrian street environment. Such experience is part of visiting many shoreline cities, such as Venice, Italy. You are lost in a human created experience with all the richness of the urban human environment: the people close up with their styles, clothes apparent racial, maybe religious indications, the windows with products and enticing services, public art and happenstance meetings. Of course, thinking about the surrounding natural environment isn't exactly front and center in your mind lost in the narrow streets of Venice or Barcelona, San Francisco or New Orleans. But take a few steps and suddenly, there is the openness of sea or

Above, the surface of the Galapagos Islands is largely a landscape of very small rolling hills, as seen here above, caused by the hardening of lava flows becoming viscose as they cool heading downslope toward the ocean, something like the flow of cooling candle wax. This creates a kind of up and down undulating landscape of one or two stories in elevation.

lake, waves instead of cobble stones, bricks, concrete or asphalt paving almost under foot. Now, there are bodies of water, meadows or farms. There may be mountains on the horizon or pressing down on town like the 21,000-foot Illimani as the spectacle that took my breath away, looming practically overhead, as seen from many buildings in La Paz, Bolivia. In the narrow streets below, having arrived in that town of few city lights in the wee hours of the night, I didn't even know the beautiful peak draped in snowdrifts and glaciers was there the night of my arrival, until the next day. I discovered this stunning mountain when I left the narrow, view-constricted streets and stepped out of an elevator in a taller building and into the in-your-face presence of that fantastic mountain.

Whatever connects us to the natural or resources base of our lives and those of the other biota deserves a good prospect always, a place for a respectful to worshipful viewing. Or perhaps through the permeable urban edge there is even the desert beyond the blooming oasis. The specific design for the urban/nature edge and opening for connection all depends on where you are. Even flat Kansas plains can be celebrated from a keyhole plaza with a view defined and framed by buildings that stress the horizontal line, as famously Frank Lloyd Wright uses it dramatically in most of his buildings.

You may experience this human/nature edge of culture up against nature also as a portal into another kind of interior, the intense interiority of a thriving forest, for example. The dormitory "villages" of the University of California at Santa Cruz, that function much like real villages, provided such a town/forest relationship when I visited way back in the early 1980s; I don't know if new development there has protected the now-getting-old arrangement of buildings and nature, or has built new in that style that is essentially small college town centers with eateries, sundries and necessities like a small drug store or country general store provides, some entertainment spaces, library/study hall… and the columns of the towering redwood trees around and even in some cases, inside the urban/village experience I enjoyed there. These immense shafts rising to a dense canopy high in the sky, punctuated by beams of light angling under, practically pressed against the dormitory windows. Just a few steps from this highly "mixed use" cultural environment – dwelling, working, studying, enjoying, eating, sleeping, friend-making, places for learning – and you cross through the permeable edge into the natural outside, which in this case, until paths take you out into pasture land, is another kind of inside.

The juxtaposition of the two experiences – the cultural place and the natural place – is important for experiencing and communicating about ecocity concepts and the concept of completeness in its own right. And the ideal place and historic context for broadcasting such change at the speed of thought, again I believe, would be – Allah and Darwin willing – the Galápagos Islands.

How the small but tall village "skyline" and relationship of human, cultural, urban, interiority could be expressed in the Galapagos, I was already thinking at Rosalia Arteaga's FIDAL house. Add the amazing views there on the Enchanted Isles, the thoroughly unique wildlife and a colorful and powerful message rich in visuals, and you are ready to broadcast the good news.

It's like this: on even as small an area as one block, a narrow pedestrian street cuts through the block, making a turn or intersecting another pedestrian street. At the intersection there are a couple of the sorts of shops elsewhere in the small towns of the islands. Shop windows, other people are passing along and you are lost in your own internal mental meanderings… nothing would seem to connect you to the great out-of-doors. Being lost in an urban experience yet with the great out of doors just a very short distance away is a situation created on a surprisingly small area of land, according to ecocity design. In fact, it should be created on the Galápagos to – face it directly – help reverse climate change and species extinctions on our home planet by waking people up to the ultimate in healthy city design and development. Learning from evolution about the lessons for city development is that big in human and nature's affairs, and of course, nothing is as big as evolution seen as the whole universe in its changes through time. As said before, we have to get it right.

Dinner for 300. The corner of Calle Indefatigable and Aveniada Baltra, where Indefatigable is soon to become a one block outdoor restaurant and street for ambling and eating. This happens every Thursday evening. Most of the time it's one way with pedestrians, bikes, taxis and last in terms of traffic flow, cars. Never much traffic while I was there, a total of about four weeks in Pueto Ayroa, Santa Cruz Island.

The other features, built into stretching a bit the average height of buildings already there on the islands and emphasizing the connection with "appropriate technologies..." and that's enough to deliver an important conclusion: "This is a big part of the solution."

One last point before moving on to the particular examples of what I think should comprise a small ecocity project or two on the Enchanted Isles. And that point is that the ecocity built project is "a silver bullet."

That term is common for one solution solving many problems all at once, a "cure all." I've never believed in such a notion. But I have recently reconsidered. There's low consensus that silver bullets exist; smart people think the idea simplistic. It's not. It can be "whole systems," the parts within united together for a crucial job, or rather, set of jobs. Some silver bullets do exist and the ecocity is one of them. Part of the reason ecocities are close to a cure all — nothing is a cure *all* after all — or at least a cure-many-problems-all-at-once, is because we are dealing with not just architecture, or transport, or land use, or basic form – 2-D or 3-D – but with the basic proper integration of all the above *and* all those things *simultaneously*. The ecocity and its transport, energy and supporting industrial systems, like the sprawl city and its transport, energy and supporting industrial systems too, are both complex integrated whole systems.

But the main difference between the car city and the ecocity is that one of the "whole systems" is wildly dysfunctional and damaging and the other potentially quite healthy, and in both cases, the problems and the solutions, be as they may be in the two fundamentally very different systems, are multiple and linked.

Take energy conservation for example. The ecocity demands far less energy, mostly for two reasons: very little is needed to run the ecocity's transportation and massive amounts are needed for the city of suburban sprawl. The second big energy consideration: relatively compact development means heating and cooling energy is shared in the ecocity mode because walls, ceilings and floors are often shared, whereas in separate houses the energy of heating and cooling is lost outward with just one use. Simply stated, per person, apartments are far more energy efficient than separate houses. OK, so you can't imagine living in an apartment. Then imagine living with severe climate change, heating and drying of most of the planet and well over a billion people dislocated by rising seas because there is no culprit more impactful than sprawling city form.

"But I live in a single-family house with big lawn and double garage and two cars."

"OK. But put it in the back of your mind and start keeping an eye out for options, including even electing pro-ecocity politicians who could provide substantial inducements to easier change." These could range from zoning regulations to higher density housing subsidies, funded perhaps by steadily rising gasoline taxes… Many possibilities if we exercise our ecocity imaginations some. Incrementally but resolutely change the game rules.

Consider recycling when thinking silver bullet. Visiting a friend's condo in Oslo, Norway about seven stories up in the air, I noticed at the end of his hall recycling slots for five classes of "waste" getting ready for reuse: paper, metal, plastic, compost and batteries. The compost (standardized compostable bags available) and the batteries were news to me at the time. In the condo, the task, in that three-dimensional context required a 12 second walk down the hall, a gravity drop to the basement and a maintenance person spending a small percentage of his or her time to gather the materials for a recycling truck. But to haul around recyclables in cars to a recycling center from scattered houses – that takes the 2,500- to 4,000-pound machine, an enormous amount of energy and many times as much time as walking the hall and the maintenance person's time making the connections below. (Approximately 4,000 pounds is the average weight of 2020 new American cars.)

What about conservation of wild and farming land, conservation of the surface of the Earth? My estimates for a fairly high level of dissemination of ecocity thinking and influence, and imagining that happening enough to become the new normal is several decades, the ecocities would be utilizing about one fifth to one tenth the land automobile/sprawl development consumes. Put your mind to it, and think in terms of the idea of access by proximity, and proximity by way of getting the design right... and the rest is pretty formulaic planning, if of a character not yet familiar.

Most basically, the shortest distance between two points is not a straight line, but moving the points close together in the design and planning stage. This has to be done first in the mind, then in official urban planning, at any scale city to village. In this "silver bullet" discussion we are talking about the ecocity's truly gigantic contribution to a much more sane and happy future than if we continue building car-dependent cities, towns and even villages.

3

Pieces of the ecocity adding up

To keep our eyes on the prize, the building of a local ecocity project while also building the idea for broadcasting the good news out and around the world from those Enchanted Isles is truly promising. I'll start my imagery with some examples already built in Puerto Ayora, the largest town on the Galápagos Islands with about 14,000 residents. I'll show good examples of the components already coming together in a truly innovative hotel already built there exemplifying, if not the full suite of an ecocity project's essential components, taking several long steps in the right direction. It's called the Hotel Mainao. It's located exactly one block into the town from the main fishers' landing facilities on Avenida Charles Darwin at the water's edge. Most obvious, though a surprise to me as I walked around Puerto Ayora for the first time: the broad and numerous roofs to shade architecture from the unforgiving local sun at the equator.

Left, three stories plus a small fourth story tower with shade roofs all the way up, a cell tower in the background. In the foreground, bikes and motor bikes are more common than cars. The roof structures for shade are emphasized here in pink. Right, circular stairs join the broad eaves adding shade on the walls, helping to cool the building's interior and also not taking up interior space.

Then we have exterior staircases of a variety of designs, circular as well as back and forth rising zig-zags, all of them casting shade and adding to protection of buildings from the sun, cooling walls somewhat, adding services in the right direction.

Above left, the view west from the unloading spot for the fishing pier on Avenida Charles Darwin. In pink for highlighting again we have the shade-providing extended roofs. Right is the landing place for fishers seen from Academy Bay, named for the California Academy of Sciences' sail ship, the Academy which collected more Galápagos animals for study than any other institution in the world. Again, pink indicates sun shading roofs.

From the simple even funky to the complex very high tech, renewable energy systems are the style on the Enchanted Isles. On the left a makeshift solution extending the roof for more shade for diners at the Tropic Bird café restaurant, which I recommend for a hearty inexpensive breakfast on Avenida Charles Darwin diagonally across from the fishing pier. Right, a technician for the island's electric company works on one of the giant wind machines near the airport on Baltra Island just north of Santa Cruz Island.
Photo on right, Newsweek Magazine.

Everywhere we walk we can see the roofs providing shade for many of the buildings. In cooler climates we have those attached solar greenhouses gathering and holding warmth into the night. They are called "passive solar:" you don't need electricity or machines to transfer water or air from place to place through mechanical intervention. Once built, such features just work. Here, with these shading roofs we have the passive cooling equivalent of passive solar heating in climates far from the equator but appropriate to this equatorial climate. These islands are generally covered by thin low clouds that prevail much of the time, but much of the sun's heat gets through. Clouds gather on the mountain tops and the windward side of the islands, the higher the islands the more prominent and frequent the clouds. They almost define the Galápagos. Occasionally they do rain – only to have the cracks in the ragged lava substrate take most of the water straight down deep into the stone interior, and, I'd surmise, to eventually leak out into the ocean horizontally as the sparse rainwater seeps down and eventually slowly out to sea. That's why there is practically no surface water flowing in streams anywhere on the islands. And that's a water problem for agriculture and drinking that we will visit later.

Above, we see, marked by colored "hat pins" on the right, six bicycles, four white taxis with pick-up box in back, three motor scooters and, crossing the relatively calm street, one pedestrian. This is Avenida Baltra named for the island where the main airport for the Galápagos islands is located about an hour north of Puerto Ayora. Notice also the nice hedge dividing the bicycle two-way street from the one-way car lane. A number of other streets in town are one-way also, the car definitely de-emphasized.

In a very real sense, when you start thinking pedestrian city, town and village, when you realize the importance of three-dimensional arrangements of the built community designed mainly for pedestrians, you begin to realize that staircases, elevators and bridges between buildings are an integral part of the transportation system, part of the "organic whole" of parts and possibly some day of virtually the whole ecocity, ecotown and ecovillage. The Galápagos have a fair number of these features… except for elevators, of which I know of only one: at the four-story Hotel Albatross on Puerto Ayora's western edge. The hotel has a feature in its contract with Mitsubishi Elevator Company that assures the hotel owners that if there is a problem with the device, a technician will be on site in less than 24 hours.

Behind this photo, above, is the story of the relatively calm and safe streets. Motor scooters there move only slightly faster than bicycles. The child looks delicately seated but if speeds there are slow, maybe it's OK that way.

Seat, foot rest and handlebars for a child on this electric scooter, left, but a friend of a friend is training his children to enjoy cars, there as almost everywhere.

Above, we have bridges on the undulating landscape of the Galápagos that comes from floods of lava on the order of ten or fifteen feet thick lying one over the other, cooling, hardening and cracking. Thus, some buildings seem to rise up from under the general surface level as in these two cases, left, bridge stairs leading into a home's second floor and another, stairs leading to the first floor. On the right, the bridge is to the entrance to the second story of the Lonesome George Hotel.

It was striking soon after arriving that not only had Puerto Ayora – and I discovered later also the town of Puerto Baquerizo Moreno on San Cristóbal Island – demonstrated that the local people were already employing an impressive variety of ecocity features, but also that much of what they were building was strikingly imaginative. I would never have guessed someone would have employed bannisters in a wide variety of forms, like crashing waves and a few handrails wiggling about like undulating snakes. Why not

Above, two of the unusual banisters of Puerto Ayora. And note the shading roofs again and shade created by the outside stairs.

bannisters you have to think about grasping with different angles of your wrist as you move up or down? They probably help keep people alert.

The Galápagos Islands economy is mostly designed around the tourist, if one generally looking for meaningful educational experiences as well as entertainment, fun and some relaxation. Some tourists look for excitement and tales of adventure to be brought back from the islands, as for example swimming with the local hammerhead sharks, who have yet to attack a human. Sounds daring and courageous though. How about sighting one of their formidable ten-inch long black centipedes, not appearing in the tourism literature, but thankfully rare, like the one I saw being chased by an enthusiastic dog. Relative to the dog, the centipede must have been two feet long relative to a six-foot person. Fortunately you see hundreds more blue footed boobies than those spooky big strings of beads with dozens of legs.

In Latin America the towns are generally more colorful – literally – than in the US, Europe, Asia or Australia, more like Africa in that regard, especially when you consider bold pattern and colors in clothing in Africa. But in the Galápagos Islands, that colorfulness is added to with more imaginative features that look to entertain and attract the evolutionary curiosity, that is colorful in even a wider spectrum than simply brighter colors. Added to the bannisters and sheltering roofs of a variety of designs, the walls, both of buildings and as space dividers around yards come in a variety of forms.

4

The Hotel Mainao,
Puerto Ayora, Santa Cruz Island

I had the great good fortune of meeting Sofia Darquea, President of the Galápagos National Park Guides and Interpreters Association. When we had the opportunity for me to explain the goal of an ecocity model project she said, "Well then you must see the Hotel Mainao. It's a cluster of several buildings linked by bridges. It's extremely imaginative and Ignacio Sangolqui, the owner of the hotel, is its designer. He speaks great English too and likes talking about the buildings. He's enormously enthusiastic for his innovations, very friendly. He's a natural architect. He'll probably take you on an amazing tour." He did.

If you are in the Galápagos looking for ecocity features you find them immediately in the form of buildings with roofs extend out over much of the particular buildings as shown earlier herein, buildings of all sorts: residential, hotel, restaurant, shops, offices and so on. Shade roofs here work for comfort like solar greenhouses do attached to buildings in cooler climates, catching and holding heat with their sunny side glass and "thermal mass." Building

The Hotel Mainao in Puerto Ayora, Santa Cruz Island is actually a set of three separate buildings four and five stories tall linked by bridges and flying stair cases. Above the reception room in the foreground and two of the buildings overlapping just behind.

materials and color of surfaces to attract and hold the heat of the sun are typical in, for example, solar passive houses around Santa Fe, New Mexico where adobe (dried mud brick) buildings are traditional. Adobe has magnificent thermal properties, holding heat and releasing it slowly, thus helping heat homes in cooler climates all night with heat gathered in the day. The soil itself in solar greenhouses helps moderate interior temperatures in temperate climates.

In the Galápagos breezy balconies also cast shade, and having some people on the balconies and people on the second or third floor terraces lends a sociable presence of people to the streets. To exterior stairs, bridges, balconies and terraces, many owners and builders there feature the colorful shading of bougainvillea-covered trellises that also protect walls of buildings.

Imagine now – and this starts getting into what should be platinum rated neighborhood design in a system like LEED building certification – linking his three buildings with bridges. But also imagine such "compound structures" headed into something like a whole functional small neighborhood with a couple restaurants or cafes, not just in-the-price break-

Above, we can see two bridges connecting two of the Hotel Mainao buildings and two stair cases under construction while other parts of the complex are open for guests.

fasts for the hotel guests, but open to the paying public as well. That's not there at the Hotel Mainao but would be in a full-on ecocity small project. Some small shops and offices, a few real apartments for locals, not just touring guests. Educational information as a big enhancement of the usual tourist brochures with the equivalent of very small exhibits in hotel lobbies of the rather fantastic flora and fauna there would all be part of an ecocity-style project on the Isles. There could be a self-conscious focus on actually educating beyond just supporting tourist curiosity by incorporating the local citizens as customers, taking advantage of the lead by the Charles Darwin Research Station in appealing to the eco-curiosity of visitors and residents

31

alike. It would be especially nice catering to children, that is, make it a very obvious approach at broad education about ecology there with even the evolutionary lessons for ecocity design. Some of that is there already. Much more could be part of the ecocity/evolution project. Why not some imagery of the pedestrian traditional village on an occasional wall, with a little explanation? A small shelf of books on all the above could feature, for example, my books on ecocities and some of the excellent, even exciting one's I've read… I know there are many out there.

Composite photo, view of Academy Bay from the Hotel Mainao.

If we are talking about a small project of say just one or two blocks, we need to be also talking about a long-range plan that encourages the remodeling and building of a collective infrastructure that knits together over a few decades, something like the way Ignacio Sangolqui has knitted together his three basic structures. That enters the realm beyond single building architecture and moves into true eco-community design. There is plenty of room for a micro street system scaled to the human measure, common enough in many European old streets, far too narrow for cars. One or two blocks are enough land area for one, two or even three narrow pedestrian "interior" streets where you are lost to the outside world and in a real urban experience.

But at that small scale on just a couple small blocks there is also room for a small plaza or two, like larger patios, that open to the views from second and third floors. Just one or two stories taller than the Hotel Mainao offers almost endless opportunities for innovations linking the people there by visual sight lines with the rest of the community and most importantly, with nature in that extraordinary location.

Build it and the attention will come. And if the attention comes, we will have a powerful educational tool for a healthier, happier future everywhere people pay attention.

Keyhole plaza

The keyhole plaza idea, above, is to surround a public gathering place with some of the town's most interesting architecture but to leave a side or a corner open to celebrate a revered local view.

5

Lynn Margulis, with Charles Darwin, completing the Theory

Now let's step back to look at evolution itself in a little more depth, and if we do that, we discover that a woman has matched Darwin in an extraordinarily powerful way, by completing the basic outline of the theory of evolution. True, evolution theory will almost certainly go on being refined and better understood deep into the future. But the big second step after Darwin's, I'm convinced, was taken by Lynn Margulis, microbiologist. And wonderful that the scientist to complete the picture is a woman, Darwin addressing the competitive dimensions of evolution and Margulis the cooperative.

Here's how I met her, in my readings, that is. First, her idea of endosymbiosis I'd run across around 2002. Since I hadn't been reading biology text books lately, back then, I didn't know her ideas were finally catching on. But in a few popular articles I learned about the basic concept.

Everyone in and beyond basic biology in high school knows about symbiosis: the living (-biosis) together (sym-) of different organisms such that the arrangement is beneficial to both. Famously, the lichen is often the first

The Origin of Eukaryotic Cells

Animal

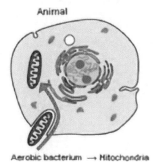

Aerobic bacterium → Mitochondria

Plant

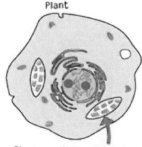

Bluegreen algae → Chloroplast

Endosymbiosis, above, simple cells become much more complex as aerobic bacterium and algae invade simple early cells. This produces the higher animals (left) and plants (right). Prokaryotic cells are the simple early cells without "organelles" inside, like the mitochondria and chloroplasts above, and eukaryotic cells are the complex ones that arise when aerobic bacterium and blue green algae get in and somehow survive, tuning their metabolism and reproduction to that of the host cell or vice versa or both.

symbiotic relationship the student learns about. A lichen is actually two beasties, one a blue-green algae, aka cyanobacteria, and one a fungus, the two tightly locked together. The algae provide energy from sunlight through chlorophyll processes building sugars, starches and cellulose, and the fungi provide a filamentous structure to hold the algae, and also help collect from the air and rain water and minerals beneficial to the metabolism of the algae.

But endosymbiosis is a truly breath-taking leap into new territory for symbiosis. And that endo-symbiosis process has resulted in the genesis of all the higher plants and animals of this planet, and that's saying a lot.

Lynn Margulis wasn't the first to propose that something very interesting might be going on very early in evolution's history. A few scientists of the microbiologist sort had long wondered where the complex cells got their inner parts, called organelles. There's the nucleus itself of these higher cells, both plant and animal, and for plants the organelles called chloroplasts busily work away building those sugars, starches and cellulose for their own metabolism and growth and providing fuel for and powering movement of the animals when the animals eat the plants with the sugars and other compounds in plants' tissues.

Those organelles, in other words, actually came from bacteria of the simple algae type or animal type seeking nourishment themselves and they got lodged inside of their prospective lunch or dinner. Or maybe got enveloped in some manner like we see when amoebas surround and eat, or try to eat, something? What if instead of succeeding at that (getting a meal), the would-be-eater is essentially enveloped by the larger party and manages to hang on, literally "in" there, using some services from the enveloping host cell, maybe living on some of its waste products? After millions of generations in the patient selective processes of evolution, goes the idea, the host cell and invader-become-guest, adjust to each other's reproductive cycles to literally become a new type of much more complex cell... What then?

"What then," turns out to be a whole new deal, a giant leap for life into new potentialities. In fact, not just potentialities but actualities of critters with countless new capabilities. Evolution could then accelerate enormously and diversify like crazy. A fabulous new level in evolution was initiated, in terms of theory, and Lynn Margulis was the main genius to recognize and work hard to bring this news about evolution to us Earthlings.

So, sometime in 2012 I decided, as I often decide, I have to go seek out and meet another amazing person, Lynn Margulis in this case. Beginning with

Lynn Margulis, champion of endosymbiosis from an uncredited Internet source

Wikipedia. I had an abrupt, rude and highly discouraging start. She had just died the year before. So, I meandered on my intellectual winding path thinking, a bit depressed, I'd run into her later in some way. Where? Among the "billions and billions of stars," to quote Carl Sagan.

I'd always enjoyed Carl Sagan and reading biographies. Put the two together and I was a few short chapters into a book about the remarkable popularizer of astronomy, space travel and "exobiology," which means the study of likely life on other planets beyond our own. Interesting guy I thought, while enjoying his television show, *Cosmos*, his books and *Contact*, the movie he scripted.

Then, just a couple chapters into his early science life unfolding, he runs into a perky young thing coming up the staircase of the Math Building at the University of Chicago. And damned if it isn't 16 year old Lynn Margulis, whose last name at the time was Alexander, who I'd been admiring for about a decade through my reading. I was startled. Here she is again! He's a pretty cute, self-confident and energetic guy bursting with enthusiasm, she immediately sees, and she's no wallflower herself. They instantly start gabbing most happily and, being in the Math Building, he takes her number.

They fall in love, get married, have two children, live near me in Oakland for a time (never met them personally) and get divorced when Lynn decides she was tired of Carl never doing the dishes or even being home to share in any way the house-keeping and child rearing. Really bad. Carl was noteworthy as very affectionate toward the boys, crawling around on the floor playing with them. But he was even jealous of his own toddling rug rat sons getting more attention than he was from Lynn, though of course he wasn't home that much. So, she pooped out on Carl, even though he was a lovely intellectual playmate no doubt, in billions and billions of ways.

Carl was blindsided; he wasn't paying attention in the right directions. She went down to the Alameda County Courthouse one long block and a half from the apartment where I was living while reading *Carl Sagan – A Life*, by Keay Davidson. She was finding it hard to get her degrees in microbiology and do all the diaper changing, cooking, sweeping, carting the two kids around, washing Carl's clothes. It was over. But it had lasted more than five years. So not all totally bad. Their conversations (other than about household responsibilities) must have been amazing.

About then, when reading the Carl and Lynn story, in the winter of 2017/2018, I heard about and read *Darwin's Ghosts – The Secret History of Evolution*. Says Rebecca Stott, its author, Mr. Darwin was upset that, with the publishing of his book *The Origin of Species*, many of his friends and colleagues felt betrayed by his omission of their influence on "Darwin's" Theory of Evolution. "Hey! We were there too," came the chorus.

Charles Darwin squirmed about, making legitimate excuses: He had to write it faster than anything else he'd ever written to make a good showing with Alfred Russell Wallace who had come up with the same theory way down in the Indonesian Archipelago. There the poor, lean and hungry young man was collecting amazing species to make a living, shipping them back to England to museums and collectors. Plus, he loved the theory in the work. Any good scientist would understand wanting "priority" on a major idea, and Charles Darwin rushed to not be surpassed by the collector way out in the field. His scientist friends would all appreciate that. Darwin was even happy to share the limelight with this inspired, respectful and kind-hearted Mr. Wallace. Darwin was also sick as usual with his various mysterious maladies, he groused. And adding a third excuse, he acknowledged he wasn't much of a science historian and would certainly leave out or give too much credit to others who came before himself so he would just simply look absent minded about and not mention his antecedents fearing he might make some real mistakes. He was in a hurry and in a word, he was interested in a tie, suggested by his two great friends, botanist Joseph Hooker and geologist Charles Lyell.

So, almost immediately after publication, he wrote his unhappy contemporary evolutionists, gentleman that he was, explaining all that. Now

Late in life Alfred Russell Wallace contemplates his distant collaborator, outliving Darwin by 31 years.

that he'd gotten over the first hump for Origin, he would credit them as best he could for helping develop the theory in his next editions of the book, and, since the whole first edition of 1,250 sold out on the first day, that would be pretty soon. The list came up to eighteen contributors in the second edition, thirty in the third edition and thirty-seven by the fourth edition. Then as he rethought the list, he started pulling a few of the fluffy ones out for even later editions.

Rebecca Stott researched scrupulously into the subject looking for scientists contributing to the theory. Her selected most important folks who followed evidence, experience and did experiments to check things out, that is, who were honest real scientists helping shape these evolution ideas, were the ones to be included on Ms. Stott's list. With modification – some additions and many deletions – Darwin's lists became members of Stott's list of significant evolutionists. She dealt with only those who preceded Darwin, being his ghosts at the time of publishing The Origin of Species, 1859. She discovered some she thought made the grade, and, like Darwin himself, winnowed out the weak ones on her list, she being more of a science historian than he was. And my reason to like "the list" idea so much is largely that when we come to know the actual hard working, risk taking, sometimes life risking, people themselves who were helping shape this "theory" becoming a complex "law" of nature, we begin to grasp how difficult, even dangerous, a new idea can be. That is, a correct-as-likely-possible view to what is actually happening in this set of dynamics we call evolution, puts a very serious yet human face on our progress if we notice for their exploring the pioneers involved. It's easier to understand if we have some idea of who came up with it, and something of their lives. Some sense of identify with those in the trenches helps.

But as said, Stott's list stopped with the publication of The Origin itself. What to do about the geneticists with their electron microscopes that came later? What about Lynn Margulis with her tremendous idea that balanced Darwin's competition with the world's highest degree of cooperation: internal symbiosis taking evolution into a wild variety of fantastic but the ever so real new forms of rich life flourishing on our planet?

Looking back, we can see these grand advances of science happening. Ptolemy's Earth-centered universe gave way to the Copernican Revolution in which we all caught on to the sun, not the Earth, being that around which the other revolves. But was that a step in evolution? Not really. The change there was from a perspective of the way it is to another perspective of the way it is, not the way it became and is becoming something different. That's evolution. And in that scientific adventure, Lynn Margulis has to be as powerful a contributor as is conceivable, right up there with Mr. Darwin and his friend Wallace. Or so I think. Competition plus cooperation equals the real deal, the complete theory, something we can work with in ordering our cities and understanding ourselves.

Rebecca Stott in Darwin's Ghosts has also focused on biological evolution almost exclusively. What about the whole pattern of evolution, including ideas of the "Big Bang" and the formation of stars and planets? The creation of heavier elements beyond hydrogen in the stars and advent of chemistry from stars that blow up in supernovas broadcasting the heavier elements into space and seeding planets? She didn't address that, but someone not on her list by the name of Pierre Simon de Laplace, for example, did somewhere around 1810. He said that long before Earth spawned life, the gases of the early universe collected together by gravitational compression forming stars. Around second-generation stars, planets also condensed out of dust and gasses of supernovas into the planets including, of course, Earth. As stars and planets evolved in three-dimensional form so did living organisms, and straight to this particular point in this book, so did cities… until cars came along and spread them out in the two-dimensional and exceedingly wasteful sprawl pattern across vast energy gobbling, atmosphere transforming, planet heating, coastline swamping landscapes for a whole planet. It is hard to grasp that but I believe it is the truth of the matter. Imagine, instead of walking across town, we all have to have a 4,000 pound block of steel, plastic, glass, rubber and millions of acres of paving and suburban lawns scattered about, and burn approximate 500 gallons of gasoline (about 15 full bathtubs) a year per person in the US to do almost anything once you plan, build and move into the suburbs.

What about cultural evolution evolving from individual consciousness evolving in humans? What about the effect the villages, towns and cities, by being created and becoming another environment for life to adapt to, becoming a force of evolution to eventually affect – already affecting – our own human evolution right down to the very genes in our flesh, probably very little so far, but on our way… to what and where? Professor William Durham of Stanford University has addressed this question of cultural evolution lodging in our genes as we adapt to fit that which we create. He gives this some fascinating attention in his book *Coevolution – Genes, Culture and Human Diversity*. The debate in all its dynamic dimensions is crucially important, especially now that cities are by far the largest of human creations and obviously designed (largely unconsciously) for enormous damage to planet Earth. Can we extract lessons from evolution to help guide city development so that we come out with a much more healthy and happy future than presently seems to be in the cards, tea leaves, crystal balls and I-Ching casting sticks?

Those that know me know I like to be specific about such lessons and just put them out there for consideration. Thus, I'm suggesting that evolution organizes complex living things in three-dimensions, not flat like the car-dependent suburbs. (I'm not the only one making this suggestion but rather following in this particular.) Something prosaic is the lesson: back off from cars and create the far more pedestrian city, town and village. Yes, I know I'm repeating myself, but an introduction to another detail: How the pieces of the built habitat fit together is as important as the arrangement of organs in complex living organisms, my "anatomy analogy:" the city *like* a normal, healthy complex living organism. Those following my newsletters and reading my recent books have heard this enough to experience yawns of over-recognition but for newcomers... write in and I'll add you to my mailing list: Ecocity World, PO Box 114 Williams, California 95987 or use ecocityworld@gmail.com.

You can also now see why I've mentioned Laplace's conclusion that stars like our sun form more or less as he thought they did, as part of evolution: those entities he was talking about, those celestial bodies, were another case of an amazingly well ordered three-dimensional coming together from a simpler, far more chaotic earlier universe, chaotic yet incredibly simple compared to what was to... evolve. That's dead center evolution theory. For the history of the genesis of the theory I recommend Stott's book.

How to update Rebecca Stott's important list? Add who we think are making basic major progress, and that would include the geneticists but again I suggest, it is hard to imagine anyone more important than she who gave us the powerful emphasis on endosymbiosis, Lynn Margulis.

6

Why me? And what must be done?

As I've suggested earlier, biographies are important, giving ideas a human face. That comes down to me and why I seem to be so interested in evolution. What's the motivation here? Why have I latched onto this ecocity theme as if I were trying to rescue a drowning person? But taking on the conversation about species evolving, including my own… I believe few things could be more important: considering what actually is evolving.

Meantime, learning from evolution as well as ecology, if not quite as emphasized, isn't really unusual since most environmentalist have nothing other in mind than what turns out to be the same thing as environmentalism. By that I mean that ecology and evolution are one in the same thing, just looked at in vastly different time periods. The same principles apply throughout, with ecology in time periods that lend understanding in looking at only a couple centuries of changes in biota, changes in geology and climate change. But with evolution we are looking at biota changing in intimate relationship with geology and climate through hundreds of millions of years, even billions of years.

So, in my case, why me? Why is it I'm bringing you these reflections and recommendations for action, to put my own human face on these seemingly abstract but actually physically grounded ideas? My background leads directly to these black glassy lava, hard-edged Galápagos Islands of natural selection. To explain myself and why this mission seems important to me, it starts with my father and his father being architects. I grew up helping layout and build my family's sequence of houses in the countryside near Santa Fe, New

Mexico and later making a fair fraction of my living building and sometimes designing construction projects, mostly in California. My father was a francophile, lover of all things French, his mother being French, taking trips there when he could. Our humble house in my grade school days, of the start-up-and-coming young architect, my father, had old photos and water colors of French villages, country scenes on the walls there: sail boats, small road bridges, Paris and other cities, farmers working fields with scythes, tables laid out with bread, wine and cheese … all things French.

My mother was a "culture vulture," my unofficial hands-off tutor providing art supplies, microscopes, telescopes, hints, &c. Our family was the only one I knew with a well-consulted encyclopedia, which cost more than one hundred bucks back when most books cost around two dollars. She loved gardening and we planted a lot together. Up it all came and we ate it. I was off to piano, guitar, cornet classes, ballroom dancing and even ballet: I was Peter of *Peter and the Wolf* and the nasty brother who broke the nutcracker in *The Nutcracker Suite*. I didn't understand why gay guys seemed only to apply when I got to throw beautiful adolescent girls up into the air and catch their shapely and magically transforming bodies.

Plus, we took two-week vacations to Mexico every year from when I was about seven to fourteen years old: cultural emersion – as much as somewhat arty tourists might do anyway. Then I was sent away to a fantastic boarding school in Arizona, a high school called Verde Valley. Our 130 students came from 20 to 25 countries the three years of my living there and we'd all pile into several trucks, covered inside their back-box interior with mats and pillows, big windows to the passing landscape, and we'd take off to Mexico every year for a whole month. We'd spend another week on the Indian reservations of Arizona. It was a teenage paradise for the intellect and body. Boy was I privileged, culturally speaking. I felt obligated to give back, maybe due partially to my mother's fundamentalist Christian beliefs somehow – like I'd be severely judged one day if I weren't grateful and giving back myself. And despite that, she was no enemy to evolution and Mr. Charles Darwin, something like Pope Francis but protestant and way ahead of the good Pope's times. She was horrified that I didn't believe in quite her version of God and Jesus. I thought if he was the Prince of Peace, what's with her support for the Vietnam war? She was a complex character. Religion and politics divided us until she was in her 90s when she finally gave up on her attempted family forcing proselytizing, then died at 94.

More to the point: why did I have a mania for trying to help our dear planet from Jr. High School age on? Why was I and my best friend in my adolescence the only two kids I knew who actually wanted to be, when we grew up, philosophers, of all things? I learned only at about age 70 that Darwin was called "Philosopher" and, most commonly, "Philos," by his shipmates on his HMS Beagle trip to the Galápagos and around the world.

But my "try-to-save-the-world" attitude may have had more to do with Los Alamos, New Mexico, the legendary "Atomic City" on "The Hill", a mountain plateau actually, across the Rio Grande River Valley from Santa Fe to the west. If you are from Santa Fe you may notice that some times of year, if you are within about 15 miles to the south to 15 miles to the north of the city, the sun, moon, stars and planets set into Los Alamos. Mars, god of war,

The nightmare of my teen years was nuclear annihilation. Here I was imagining, above, just how much larger – 1,000 times larger – the hydrogen bomb was compared to the one dropped on Hiroshima, closer to us and represented in the lower right corner.

the planet being red anyway, turns into a radiant glowing coal as it sets on Los Alamos many times every year. We had family friends up there, John and Elizabeth Northrup, good enough friends that my parents, my younger sister and I, when I was around twelve years old, would sometimes visit and stay overnight. They had a bomb shelter that freaked me out somewhat – way down *below* their basement. "If we take anything but a direct hit, we'll be fine," said John. In good capitalist fashion they had a Monopoly board game down there.

Their jobs, both of them: actually designing the latest most ferocious of thermonuclear (hydrogen) bombs.

Meantime, or just a little later, high school age, I'd taken to sitting on the roof of my family's hobby ranch house seven miles south of Santa Fe, with a horse for my sister. I'd sit there with my guitar playing lonely cowboy laments watching Mars burn its way into the edge of mountains in the skies over Los Alamos. I'd taken to noticing the rich and powerful, the influential, the politicians and opinion makers, all of them seemed focused mostly on getting richer and more powerful and/or famous. Who was taking care of the planet? I wasn't interested in getting rich and powerful but I'd certainly like to have a happy life exploring life, become well known enough and respected and have a cosmic ecstatic time with some "girls" as I was coming into sexual thoughts about then and *not* die in a swirl of burning heat, radiation and nuclear shock wave. The mushroom cloud image terrified me. I had nightmares that one such black radiation cloud would eat me up. In a split second.

By weird coincidence, only five years ago or so I sat next to an old Korean gentleman on a jet plane from Incheon, Korea to Narita Airport just outside Tokyo. He was a Korean child living in Hiroshima in 1945 when he was growing up. I found that out in random discussion. A chill went down my back.

I asked. Yes, he saw the Hiroshima bomb explode from his grade school only about a mile and a half away, the most beautiful thing he ever saw, at eight years of age, swirling radiant colors rising in silence into the air after an intense flash. He had a few seconds to really watch it. Then the deafening shock wave hit, just as I'd imagined it would as a teenager, but he was lucky. The school was new, it was summer, and to save money – wartime economics – the windows had no glass in them yet, just the wooden frames, so no razor splinters blew out to fly into his amazed eyes. It turns out he's now one of the world experts on neutrinos, those elusive tiniest of particles that can penetrate and pass through the entire Earth without hitting anything. He said look him up in *A Different Universe – Reinventing Physics from the Bottom Down* by Nobel Laureate Robert Laughlin. Sure enough, there he was, Chung-Wook Kim.

Maybe with Jesus as an oblique influence, someone trying to save the world – I was more a philosopher already compared to a religious person, yet here too a child of my mother's – I'd have to ply my imagination to try my best and beat Armageddon and give salvation to the planet. I believed everyone should try to do that, otherwise what is democracy all about? Put your energy out there and try to improve things. We can all contribute. I believe it is even our democratic duty.

7

Soleri and de Chardin – I cross paths with evolution ideas

When I thought through the threats coming to bear upon us, by the time I was 21 I'd come to believe that a very large part of saving the world would have to be building cities that were not contributing massively to planetary destruction. My Influence there was Teilhard de Chardin, Catholic priest and philosopher of evolution thinking and Paolo Soleri, architect and experimental city-builder who I had met that year, 1965, both of them, by the sheer coincidence of catching a ride hitchhiking. My host said, "Do you mind if we visit a famous architect...?" I said, "Certainly not. Sounds interesting." Thus I got myself semi-self-chosen to do this work of "ecocity" design. (I could have said, "No thanks. I try someone else. I'm in a hurry.")

De Chardin spoke of the evolution of all things in a pattern of miniaturization and complexification through time. Soleri pointed out this had everything to do with cities being redesigned around short walkable distances, miniaturized distances, in a three-dimensional pattern of the sort that makes ecological sense and fits snuggly into the patterns that seem to work for all complex living entities. I've ended up calling this the "anatomy analogy" – cities *like* complex living organisms. Its commanding axiom: the shortest distances between two points is not a straight line but rather designing those points close together. I also call that principle "access by proximity."

Some haven't thought much about that evolutionary sequence as a universal pattern, in fact probably one of the few master commandments of the matter/energy, space/time universe. A quick review shows scattered hydrogen gas in the early universe pulling together by incredibly minute gravitational force per atom into stars that are far, far smaller than the vast regions of space from which their matter condensed. So, the first step in the evolutionary sequence is from gas to stars. The stars cook up most of their elements in their high temperature, high pressure interiors as swirling floods of matter driven by convection currents like one sees in boiling water, but enormously larger in scale and almost inconceivably hotter in temperature, hot enough and under such pressure as to craft most of the elements in the natural universe through thermonuclear fusion.

So, it goes from hydrogen to stars. Then, when the largest stars exploded in supernovas, they seeded the galaxies with the heavier elements, which of course they are still doing. The products of these supernovas in turn gather by gravity again, but this time largely in the planets, moons, asteroids, comets, dust and more gasses. Thus stardust and raw gasses, the material for... building us life forms included. Note the stars and planets are about as 3-D as possible being spherical, and internally more complex than anything else that came before them in the evolutionary sequence.

Then living organisms appear on at least one planet, and living organisms are radically more complex and miniaturized than their planets.

Then consciousness appears in us living animals and gets pretty darn complex and so miniaturized it's hard to find *inside us* – ask psychologists and sociologists. But there it must be if it does what we do. And largely what we do, in fact the largest thing we do, is build cities. And we risk destroying them in other large activities called wars. Plus we have – also largely sprawl city related – heating of a whole planet and the changing of its climate, level of its oceans, &c, through the miniaturized to almost nothingness of thought, both in individuals and collectively in cultures, civilizations and species-wide. We build our built communities, fire up their technologies and, presto, along with fascinating action of countless sorts, also climate change, species extinctions and other problems for which we badly need solutions.

The formulaic way of looking at miniaturization/complexification in evolution, as also applied to cities, is to notice that sprawl development is actually essentially flat, that major theme you've run into in these pages several times by now. In addition, the city of cars and sprawl is gigantic, ironically, compared to the compact city. Phoenix, Arizona, say, or any other typical American automobile-dominated city compared to maybe Barcelona or Paris or New York with its Manhattan skyscrapers. I say "ironically" because the pieces seem so small, the single-family homes, the little cars, almost invisible from hilltops outside of town, swarming around like ants all lined up, seething about and busy.

Said Soleri in his lectures in those days around when I met him, in the

1960s, you look out over the scattering of these small houses and not very tall suburban business developments and shopping centers so typical in the US and you should realize that it is a gigantic infrastructure in which, instead of sharing walls, ceilings and floors as in apartments, big office buildings and so on, there is a vast number of smaller buildings that do not share these structural elements. They release the energy of heating and cooling after one use only, out to the great outdoors. The distances created by sprawl layout require enormous sheets of concrete and asphalt to try to hold things together, not to speak a massive number of automobiles and rivers and lakes of fuels to power it all. Pipes and wires for water, gas and electricity and land line connections for telephones and other links stretch great distances in the sprawl pattern as compared to distances in the more compact cities. Garages, double and sometimes triple, are often the largest room in the house.

Add it all up… to a real disaster for nature when the impacts are carefully considered. Loss of land for other uses and climate change are just the typical, and should be understood as harms, of this way of building. The wasted time and money for cars, paying for their purchase, fueling, insuring, upkeep, parking tickets, hospital and mortuary bills after accidents and the total costs of other associated demands and impacts of the car/sprawl infrastructure is just plain enormous. With crime, slums, and traffic congestion, smog and other problems all adding up to pretty dire conditions, most people considered "the city" to be in real trouble back when I met Soleri. To which he often responded in those early days of ecocity thinking: "not only are cities in bad shape, they are the *wrong* shape." He meant flat, built for cars zipping about on wheels instead of people on their feet.

Paolo Soleri working on one of his half domes which he calls his apses at Cosanti, his studio/residence/workshop in Phoenix, Arizona. He was doing exactly this when I met

48

him, and dressed this way too. The photo is from somewhere lost to my memory, though similar ones appear in the Archives of his experimental city, Arcosanti, Arizona. The picture may have been taken by my traveling companion and hitchhiking host Hatti Von Bretton. Or possibly his photographer friend who was also there at the time, Annette del Zoppo.

I asked Paolo, around 1966, how he came up with the idea that cities needed to be organized far more three-dimensionally. He said that ten years earlier he was working on a project to arrange a hypothetical city for an Arizona mesa top. His city was divided into zones of various discrete activities: residential, business, manufacture, education... But everything seemed too far apart given the large variety of functions most of us modern humans seem to want as options, even think of as necessities in our lives. Then rather suddenly he said, his enormous spread out drawings felt like stretched out and straining sheets of rubber. Then the whole idea of Mesa City just seemed to spring together in his mind, the layers of different activities one on top of the other instead of spread over large distances side by side.

Presto – the most basic of ecocity principles. Paolo would call it "arcology" rather than "ecocity," combining the words architecture, being an architect, with ecology. I've preferred "ecocity" to stress that we are talking about the whole built community, cities, towns, even villages not just a single or many single buildings. Also, arcology in his usage indicates a single-structure, a city in a building, even if one opened up to light and breezes. I believe the ecocity needs the density but not necessarily to be literally a single structure. It can be many structures united in various ways all better than by cars and their infrastructure and energy support systems.

I asked him, when he understood that the sane and radically improved city was a case of 3-D arrangements being far more efficient and healthy than 2-D. In other words, when did he realize that's what evolution seemed to be modeling? I prefaced the question saying I'd always been interested in the creation of new basic ideas and noticed Newton said he came up with the formula for gravity relaxing under a tree thinking about the fruit falling. Charles of Charles's gas law of the relationship of temperature, pressure and volume came to him when he was so relaxed he was even asleep. He kept a notepad by his bed for recording dreams and said he saw the formula first in a dream.

Paolo commented that that was interesting because his Big Notion came to him in similar relaxed circumstances. He said his wake-up call came while working on Mesa City. At about that time he was reading Teilhard de Chardin's writings describing the basic pattern of evolution moving toward more complexity and miniaturization through time. He said it occurred to him, while lying on a cot, on an afternoon break in the work day called a siesta in the Southwest US, while almost drifting off to sleep. He then very suddenly realized this pattern in evolution called for exactly the form of the city he was beginning to focus on and explore.

I said, "that must have made you feel good."

"Feel good?" he said. "I was ecstatic."

But something is missing from that scenario. Can you guess? The fact that not just consciousness but conscience should be recognized as two dimensions of the whole thing evolving, which I call conscienceness. I came to consider that we can't understand the full dimensions of our awareness without the dynamic of human care and compassion based on conscience integrated seamlessly with consciousness – observation, experiment, logic… – into its whole experience and expression: conscienceness.

This becomes a very interesting thing to think about. When the 20th century was drawing to a close and the 21st was nigh, we all suspected that Time Magazine would upgrade it's "Person of the Year" to "Person of the Century." Who would it be? My dear friend Nancy Lieblich, perceptive Montessori teacher of two and a half- to six-year-olds said, "It's going to be between Einstein and Gandhi, and Einstein will win."

Right she was. Of course. We are lost in consciousness, which is after all a magnificent place to be. But why not equal valuation for conscience? Shouldn't Gandhi's non-violence for peace, the moral quest, the inward view to the soul of the person and the species, be understood as at the roots of

Time Magazine selected Einstein as Person of the 20th Century, but as pioneer of the Theory of Evolution we might elect Darwin as Person of Forever.

attempts for justice and law? While consciousness has its math and physics, rate at least equal to Einstein's amazing knowledge of the ways of the material universe, shouldn't "the heart" join "the head" for a thorough perspective on evolution of… what? Conscienceness in the universe as experienced and evolving in us humans. Some animals can get close; you can see their sometimes compassion for their friends and family, but it is up to us humans to explore what it means to be in our position, realizing that its conscienceness evolving, not just consciousness.

We need to get things right and I'd say pretty much co-equal in importance with getting rid of war as the highest injustice is reshaping cities for the long haul, for evolutionary time in other words. Law has been a great attempt for establishing some level of justice. For justice, including for our other than human life forms on Earth, we now need laws – and life ways and habits and *habitats too* – such that we build ecocities and cease the enormous destruction visited upon all the biosphere, and even the climate system of a whole planet, largely by cities of the wrong shape: flat and automobile-dependent.

We can get there with zoning and other regulations to help ecocities happen – law applied for making cities maximally healthy and happy. Plus accessing the most imagination and creativity at our disposal. As to best place for putting forward the message, I'd offer the notion of the Galápagos Islands as the most charismatic, potentially most dramatic and effective place for a model project or two. Along with the kind of regulations to help it all happen.

In the context just mentioned, we need to cease the war against nature, and a gigantic piece of that action is all about how we build cities, towns and villages, our collective home that I'm absolutely certain can be radically improved.

8

US vs. European models – think ecotropolis

Probably the easiest way to imagine this is comparing the sprawling American automobile suburbs with the old European compact small cities and towns where everything is close together. In many places there, people lead prosperous lives, often with far more grace and style than do American suburbanites, consuming about one fifth as much land, energy and building materials.

Wait a minute! One fifth? That means even before instituting best of recycling, installing insulation and other "green" practices, we could, by our reconsidered urban layout, *start* with a savings of 80% over the current automobile/suburban model of land, energy and many other things. Remember the simple drawing of cities of three different densities on page 13. It's a radically good number, 80%, what's called a significant number. Then add to that the kind of ecocity features and functions you are now getting used to in this short book. This 80% can get us off to a great start, a gigantic contributor to a much healthier future.

To flesh this out as full-on ecocities, we could then add into the mix bicycles and streetcar systems, solar passive and active energy systems and restoration of natural habitat adjacent civilization. Buildings would be linked three-dimensionally between their rooftops and terrace gardens and restaurants by bridges as suggested earlier herein. Plazas near the edges of towns, also as suggested earlier in this book, could leave a side or corner open to celebrate views to much-appreciated natural features like mountains, coastlines, rivers, farming landscapes, and so on: my "keyhole plazas." Or the architecture could emphasize the horizon line in the environment with horizonal lines of the architecture of the more three-dimensional town.

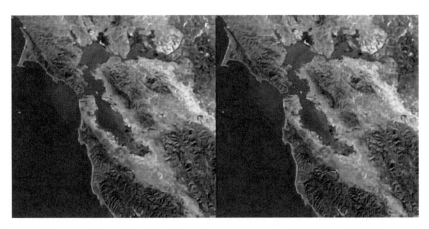

These two images of San Francisco Bay, above, come to us, left, from a NASA space satellite photo, and on the right, we've found the main city centers, district centers of smaller population and neighborhood centers that might be quite small and cozy. These two images constitute the first step in an "ecotropolis mapping system."

Above left, water rises about three feet, expanding San Francisco Bay: caused by climate change, before humanity figures out how to reverse global heating. While we are seeing increased density of the urban centers in the pedestrian mode, supported by bicycles and transit, we are also seeing a long-term return of paved-over suburban areas to natural and agricultural open space. On the right we imagine a map guiding the ecotropolis transition for Oakland, California on the east shore of San Francisco Bay. The red and orange centers get more density, diversity of facilities and functions while green is where nature and food raising return. Purple is industrial and airport uses. Wavy blue lines are restored waterways, small creeks.

Whole metropolitan areas could... *should* become ecotropolis areas, with downtowns becoming higher density ecocities, medium-sized district centers becoming ecotowns and neighborhood centers becoming ecovillages.

At the same time, nature and agriculture open up as asphalt and concrete paving, monoculture grass lawns and one- and two-story housing is being withdrawn to reveal soils that can be enriched by composting organic wastes.

How to withdraw from car-caused sprawl? Systematically with the support of policy, land trust strategies and developers building more in one place while removing development elsewhere for density bonuses by zoning law tied also to supporting highly mixed-use development. Where low density buildings burn down accidentally (or maybe otherwise too), are damaged by earthquakes, nibbled to death by termites, beetles or dry rot, or succumb to deferred maintenance or sheer aging to the point of needing replacement, *they* are *not* replaced. Instead, development rights are sent somewhere else where replacement or new construction augments the designated centers of development according to ecotropolis mapping. The standard tool for this is called a Transfer of Development Rights – TDR.

Such zoning is easily enough designed to create the ecocity centers of any stand-alone town or whole metropolitan area – *if* we decide we want ecologically healthy development and are willing to spend the time and focused thought for that purpose. The reshaping is then incremental, property by property through zoning design, or in larger chunks created by developers, either for profit or for social and ecological purposes through land banks and non-profit affordable housing organizations and so on.

By whatever legal mechanisms, many of which can be designed if we know what it is we are trying to build, we therefore need some models. Where best to build them and connect them to lessons from both ecology and evolution? Hard to beat the Galápagos Islands. Thanks for the help Mr. Darwin, good start. Good start?! Magnificent launch for the theory of evolution. We should capitalize on that.

9

The ecocity, the world holiday and the Galápagos Islands – what's the connection?

At first glance this will appear to be out of left field. First of all, what's a "world holiday"? Second, what does it, or any sort of holiday have to do with ecocities, much less the Galápagos Islands?

I have an interesting relationship to Earth Day and Denis Hayes. He was the organizer of the first Earth Day, a real wake up call for the environment to the whole world in 1970, and he is presently as I write leading much of the organizing for the 50th anniversary Earth Day, April 22 of 2020. He is the same Denis Hayes who agreed to speak at the conference I was organizing to be held on the Galapagos, scheduled for December 8 though 11 of the year of this writing, 2019. He was also my Keynote speaker at the First International Ecocity Conference in 1990. That event with 775 participants was held in Berkeley, California and lead to twelve more such ecocity conferences around the world, with a 13th in Vancouver in October, 2019. #14 is planned for Rotterdam, the Netherlands. Who knows, they may go on almost forever. Good news deserves to be heard.

I'd met Denis in 1969 shortly before the end of the year. It was on the telephone discussing an idea I had just been brainstorming, this one: the world holiday. I thought a good name for it might be World Life Day. Could such an event, a sort of environment and peace day, for everyone on the planet including the plants and animals, actually be organized into existence?

Denis Hayes, lead organizer of Earth Days 1970 and 2020. Uncredited photo from the internet, widely circulated.

Could that particular event be a powerful medium for good messages, for *good in general?* Could humanity create an event for genuinely all of us humans regardless of religion or nationality? I thought I'd explore the feasibility of the notion. Even then I was imagining a world holiday would be a major means to get the word out about reshaping our cities for a healthy future, among many other good things. A mutual acquaintance, knowing that Earth Day was in the planning for four months later suggested I talk with Denis.

Since then Denis has gotten the ball rolling and Earth Day is becoming the good solid beginning of *The* World Holiday – for all of us. So, I thought, why not ask Denis if he would like to connect all that on the Galapagos Islands and broadcast that part of the good news from Darwin's cradle of the Theory of Evolution? Denis, sometime in the summer of 2017, said yes. He'd be there and would much enjoy touring the islands some – he considered the Galápagos to be on his "bucket list." Here's the story.

For Christmas in 1969 Kirsten Weimann, my love then and still my great friend, and I had decided to go from Los Angeles back to Santa Fe, New Mexico where I had grown up. We planned to visit my high school friend Michael Mouchette. We had with us our ten-month old son Aldous, an easy and ever curious traveling companion.

When we got there, I quickly went sour on Christmas. Next door to Michael's house was a Cadillac dealership with a big gold Cadillac wrapped in a giant red ribbon in the showroom window. To the west, pouring in over the Jemez Mountains (pronounced HAY-mez, where Los Alamos rises and Mars sets) was a black/brown layer of dense smog. I was shocked. "What's *that?*" I almost gasped. "That's the new Four Corners coal-fired power plant," said Michael. "It's brand new."

Two or three days before Christmas found us taking a sightseeing drive south to near Albuquerque, then looping west and up directly north into the Jemez Mountain range, a circular rampart covered in dark blue-green pines with a vast grassy caldera in the center. Ant-sized cattle grazed in the weird optical illusion caused by the bowl-shaped crater's landscape and enormous distances up there shortly after sunset.

Driving through Los Alamos, birthplace of the atomic bomb, as twilight was darkening from purple to black, Michael driving and myself to his right, Kirsten and Aldie in the back seat, I rather off-handedly said, "I wonder what a *real* holiday would be? A holiday for all of us. Every nation, race, religion or philosophy, every animal and plant too. Maybe it would be called something like Life Day…" We noticed right away that the world *holos*, Greek for "all," was the likely root of the words health, whole, holiday, holy. I hung on to the idea for a while.

We discussed what great educational/propaganda devices holidays are. They not only deal with words, rationales, instructions for appropriate thinking and so on, sharing stories and lessons for social guidance, writing and singing celebratory songs, but they involve people in physical activities like gift giving on "the subject," visiting family, holding feasts. In old Santa Fe tradition, for example, building tiny welcoming fires in front of house thresholds is a Christmas tradition. For the world holiday we'd be doing things dedicated to bringing peace, like working to get out of the Vietnam War at the time. Maybe hosting a foreign exchange student and planning a day-long celebration for him or her. We'd be planting trees and food gardens. Recycling things, restoring healthy natural environments, working against pollution in many ways… Lots of activities would fit. Different cultures would have different things to offer. How about talking about ecocities, even founding them, laying their cornerstones?

What day of the year to choose? I didn't have any clear idea yet. But it suddenly struck me as something that might stir up some serious debate and, who knows, might actually seed the real deal: a special day, with attached season of preparing, implementing, enjoying and evaluating, then lingering on memories and lessons from… the world holiday. The next day I was writing down notes about what I might be able to do to explore the feasibility of the idea.

Two or three days after Christmas, back in Los Angeles I got in touch with columnist Art Seidenbaum who had the daily column in the Opinion Section who said, "Excellent idea, World Life Day. I'll write a column on it." Which he did almost immediately. He also said, "I know a guy who was recently hired by Senator Gaylord Nelson to organize a big national teach-in on the environment this coming spring. Would you like to talk with him? I'll be in touch with him if you like."

"Of course I'd like to talk with him."

Celebrate Earth Day – on its way to becoming the world holiday? Picture above, previous page, is from the website of Earth Day Network, with Denis Hayes, one of the major organizers of Earth Day activities in 2020. Of course, we can all do whatever we think appropriate.

It was only a day or two before I heard from Denis. As it turns out, in the intervening 50 years, Denis has actually almost created – with a lot of help from his friends – the world holiday, which is… the embryonic, or maybe being born?... Earth Day. The main issue in his phone call to me at the end of 1969 was this: should we keep the issues of the environment separate from the then current anti-war activities, simply skip the anti-war/peace issue?

To be effective, we'd need to keep a strict focus on environmental issues, he believed. We agreed we didn't want people to get freaked out by bringing up that forbidden subject of a serious confrontation with war itself, as if nationalism insists on calling that option always open, the option for nations and revolutionaries to "legitimately" go to war…, the peace issue. Despite that environment-only approach, which I believe was very effective, the anti-war debate has always been there in the background and occasionally dealt with to some degree on Earth Days. It is not like it was totally forgotten but not emphasized enough to bring out the hawks and a really gigantic reaction against the events and the organizers of Earth Day themselves. Only the most block-headed and ignorant called Earth Day activists Communist subversives or unpatriotic tools of outside agitators. Almost everyone was happy to deal with issues we all knew were real.

I mention this now in this small book as it is being written in late 2019.

Earth Day 2020 will be celebrated on April 22nd 2020 and in the days leading up to and following. It will in all likelihood be the largest event in human history, involving probably over two billion people over several days, and if Denis has his way, it will define the whole spring season of 2020. Will it be the birth of the world holiday? A couple Earth Days have topped a billion participants already. Earth Day 2020, with a full court press could make this 50th anniversary Earth Day a real planetary point of inflection in human history. It might just involve more people than any religious or national holiday on the planet ever, including Christmas and Chinese New Year.

And I mention something else in the same breath, which is that I had arranged for Denis and several other uniquely qualified pioneering environmentalists, policy makers and urban and architectural designers and also scholars on the Galápagos Islands to present at a conference planned for early December 2019 in the run up to the 50th anniversary Earth Day.

But, to make a long story short, I failed to arrive at sufficient pledged sponsorship. No serious money appeared to proceed with the Galápagos conference. There was no way to continue. So here I am writing about it instead of being there working on the event itself. Well, one step back, but hopefully this book will help us to two steps forward later on down the calendar.

When I realized I just couldn't raise the money, I was thoroughly shocked. It was the first (and so far, only) time I failed to pull off a conference I was trying to organize. For a few weeks after facing my failure I was not a little depressed since I believed – and still do – that these ideas connecting evolution, city design and planning with the lessons in your face from the living creatures of the Enchanted Isles, direct from Darwin's self-described "cradle of the Theory of Evolution," were so powerful success was inevitable. I thought there was no way the money would not materialize as it had for all my past conferences over the preceding 40 years. Those included several in addition to the ones in the International Ecocities Conference series.

But the "way" had its own way of thinking and only a few good friends and my now-departed savings account paid for initial exploration of the idea and my two trips to the Enchanted Isles. The amount for the event, approximately $120,000, medium size compared with some of my past conferences, was not gigantic and relative to the importance and the potential reach of the message must have been one of the highest leverage projects, investment-to-benefit-return, conceivable: world-wide and deeply meaningful.

That particular effort with its exquisite timing and connection through Denis to Earth Day is dead and gone, but the ideas therein… not by a long

Two scenes from the island of Floreana, it's largest volcano and mosses and bromeliads on the scalesia trees there, in the same family as the daisy but much larger.

shot. "My" International Ecocity Conferences continue onward with the thirteenth held in October, 2019 in Vancouver, Canada, probably several months or years, before you will be reading this and about three months after I finally gave up on that particular Galápagos conference.

But the wonderful opportunity of the conversation being enriched immeasurably by creative and dedicated people on site on the Enchanted Isles, and if not a major theme of the 50th Anniversary Earth Day, continues on, even if I missed that out-bound train. Other events and even building something there in the Galapagos Islands remains a possibility, for sometime in the hopefully not too far off future. The sooner the better for the health of the planet. Of that I am absolutely certain. If it can actually be done.

What this brings up for us now is back to the basic ideas in this book. Earth Day has enjoyed a growing base of support. Some of my friends have groused that it has become too commercial. All the more reason to raise the bar, and include ecocities as a major emphasis on Earth Days into the future, whether part of Earth Day events, 2020 or not. And forever, being about evolution, the city will be like the neglected child there glaring intensely at us needing attention and will continue needing attention on all future peace on Earth, peace *with* Earth Days.

Ecocities should be one of the most important themes of Earth Day 2021 and on, and where better connected to evolution than on the Galápagos Islands? If not in time for this one coming in 2020, be big for the next 50 Earth Days. Evolution and ecocities – the time for understanding these two enormous issues has to be coming.

Maybe it's OK for Earth Day 2020 to give up on big new issues, and maybe we should just round out the first 50 years in the spirit of my first phone conversation with Denis Hayes. That is, with omitting a strong emphasis on issues of war and peace, and not emphasizing ecological city design as the commanding necessity it really is. We didn't even mention ecocities since the idea was barely being born at that point in 1970. People would have said, "Eco-*whats?*" Or, "*What*-kind of cities?"

But Earth Day is well on its way in building a powerful tradition; isn't it secure and established enough to take on a little risk and broaden its ambition by challenging the legitimacy of war? As the legitimacy of slavery has been confronted and pretty near totally disappeared, so should war be eliminated while we are at the same time beginning to build all-out ecocities. Isn't the time drawing near when we have to recognize the power and helpfulness of the ecocity concept? Maybe Earth Day needs a kick in the butt by 2021, create a new point of inflection, a serious renaissance. Maybe it will be the project of the next 50 years.

That should be the challenge for Earth Days 51 through 100, to Earth Day 2070 when everyone on the planet should be celebrating from babies to hundred-year-olds, with the only holdouts being the worst of curmudgeons, grinches and scrooges, and, maybe some meditators in caves who never read the papers, or do emails, or Google searches. And the two new big themes for the next 50 Earth Days after this coming one: the illegitimacy of war, and, the reformulating of our cities, towns and villages to actually help evolution along.

All this may seem a little "out there," but the big lesson of ecology, not to speak evolution, is where we note we are all part of the same "Tree of Life," in that everything is connected. As pioneering mountaineer, naturalist poet and wilderness evangelist John Muir said, "When we try to pick out anything by itself, we find it hitched to everything else in the Universe."

And with that I leave the subject of the largest possible communications forum conceivable, at least for this planet, the world holiday, and the possibility of it and ecocities being a winning combination somehow grounded way out in the Pacific on the Galápagos Islands busy broadcasting "S.O.S, listen to this."

10

Project at the University San Francisco de Quito campus

The ideas are great, but what is it going to look like? And can we plan to build something and launch it running along healthy and happy? I'd suggest we pick two places and two projects on two separate islands of the Galápagos Archipelago, the better to flesh out some varied details.

Puerto Baquerizo Moreno on San Cristóbal Island is the Administrative Capital for the Island chain, located closest to South America and its commanding mother country, Ecuador, the only country in the world to call our planet "Mother Earth" in its political Constitution. Poets and native environmentalists must be rife there. There's a campus of the University San Francisco de Quito just a short walk to the north of the town, only a mile or two from where Darwin first landed on the islands. It's main welcoming building is back a couple dozen yards from a beautiful beach where seals and

View from just across the street in front of the University San Francisco de Quito looking west — sunset view — over the beach called Playa Mann.

humans lounge about together, and up slope maybe fifteen feet or so from mean high tide. There's an ocean view to the west to the rest of the archipelago, invisible just barely over the visual horizon. The University offers students "four Academic Tracks in the biological and social sciences: (1) Evolution, Ecology and Conservation; (2) Marine Ecology; (3) People, Politics and the Environment and (4) Sustainable Tourism." The program is international and in English with a requirement of a Spanish class as well if you don't speak Spanish. The offering looks like it could easily adopt a number of ideas and maybe local case study degrees related to ecocities fitting well within their mandate. I wish I could afford to be a student or teacher there! Seriously do! This book would then be expert instead of theory. There would be courses in ecocities. I'd get myself hired on as a visiting professor.

That USFQ campus will serve for this exercise – or an expansion of it to the north and east anyway. Several people I met there used the initials in referring to the town of Puerto Baquerizo Moreno so I will call it the PBM project, to clearly distinguish it from one I will place in Puerto Ayora.

The other location I'll just call the Puerto Ayora project. That would be on Santa Cruz Island the largest town among the four Islands that actually have towns, with Santa Cruz Island nestled into the middle of the archipelago, the naturally centrally located tourist capital for the islands. From there you can get anywhere and pretty quickly. And by the way, the boats generally used between the islands – for about 15 to 20 passengers – are powerful and fast, a bit bone jarring slamming into the waves and swells with big wings of spray erupting beside your stern and leaving a foaming pair of white trails behind. But on my four trips between islands, no one got seasick.

My guess is that because there is virtually no sideways sway and long rocking dips at those speeds the dizziness and upset stomach is much less likely to be an issue.

But back to our main line of thinking… Puerto Ayora has a population of about 13,500. Puerto Baquerizo Moreno on San Cristóbal has about 5,400 residents. For this ecocity project exercise I'll set the project in Puerto Ayora somewhere on the main street, Avenida Charles Darwin, with a view out to Academy Bay, the small unoccupied Santa Fe Island about fifteen miles out and the pacific horizon beyond.

Both projects require policy changes for municipal governments in some zoning and related regulations. Both projects are hypothetical with no official political backing at present, though some people who live there with a basic introduction to the concepts involved and that know there is an effort to study and even promote an ecocity project there, like the thinking and have had a number of good suggestions for progress. These folks have met me and some, including Darren Sears, an accomplished landscape architect with degrees from both Stanford and Harvard, have contributed valuable thinking to the project. Darren joined me in meetings and travel around the islands. In addition, we do know that the people of the Galápagos Islands and the government of Ecuador have been unusually open to and advanced in their evolutionary thinking in any case. That's evidenced by the fact that 97% of the total land area of the Galápagos Islands is reserved in as natural an environment as possible, all part of the National Park System of Ecuador.

Above. On trips between the Islands, you barely get wet at all. You are moving so fast the water is spit and thrown far to the side. Daren Sears, who joined me on the islands, is on the right with two other travelers between San Cristóbal and Santa Cruz.

That human development projects, including farming, can only occupy 3% of the islands' landscape, is a truly remarkable statistic. This and other exemplary policies were established after almost two centuries of introduced invaders – pigs, goats and cats among the most damaging. Meantime the hunting of animals like the giant tortoises for food by pirates and whalers and a handful of lonely and generally bizarre early settlers, many of whom *wanted* to be lonely, was going on. That's a whole other fascinating story. It's too much for this small book, if scandalously curious, but maybe worth looking into for a case in human *de*volution should you readers be interested. Not to mention the scientists collecting specimens starting with Mr. Darwin, himself continuing the tortoise-eating trend in 1835, then going on well into the twentieth century. For a while all the above contributed to the decimation of some of the rare or completely unique species there. The California Academy of Sciences, home of a truly magnificent museum in San Francisco's Golden Gate Park, has the world's largest collection of specimens from the Galápagos. They don't do that kind of thing anymore.

Puerto Baquerizo Moreno first. The USFQ campus has about a half dozen buildings with administrative offices and classrooms. Google Earth makes them appear linked with adjoining roofs (thus my count is a bit tentative). The folks in the offices just inside the front door didn't want me exploring the place. OK, be that way; I'm into the general functioning in any case and can use some of my own imagination. In thinking through the "massing" of buildings for different complementary functions being close together, you don't have to know exactly where each "use" goes if you know approximately the volume of space required. Thus, a part of the overall design that could be subdivided into, say, classrooms, might later be assessed, with more detail on the workings of the whole, and instead end up as apartments for, for example, student and teacher residences. The more critical element is the particular mix of uses in the massing of structures, the space per function therefore called for relative to the educational and research missions of the school. The particular proportions and harmony of relationships of the parts relative to each other and local sustainability is the main objective.

But I did look longingly at the windscreens and the umbrellas casting nice shadows up on the porch above the front doors. Though I could run up

Above and across the street from the beach, we have the entrance to the main building of the University San Francisco de Quito campus at Playa Mann just north of Puerto Baquerizo Moreno, with a blue footed booby sculpture celebrating recycling and made of recycled plastic.

the stairs in less than five seconds to check out the vista, I'm not the sort to play such games with legitimate authority. Those shaded tables and chairs would be overlooking the gorgeous beach. But with a couple very nice cafes lazily serving up food next door, on the town side of campus, I'd hang out there for a while. If the gate keepers weren't going to grant me a tour or a pass, I'd just enjoy myself studying a little Spanish under a better provision of shade and have a bite to eat next door. Sandwiches were on offer but I ordered something Latin with fish, spicy beans, fresh fruit and a beer, nice and icy. It was relevantly named Endimica, imported from as far away as Puerto Ayora, from Santa Cruz Brewery two and a half hours away by fast boat. Its label features an image of the iconic 450 foot high twin rocks just off San Cristobal's coast called Kicker Rocks, with the slender one of the two rocks now a great beer bottle silhouetted against the sky in the rolling sea. The label, with a touch of humor, didn't detract: good beer.

A small four-year-old boy took pity on me and we decided then and there the Spanish class was on. His waitress mother smiled as he jumped up on my lap and launched into the informal lesson. He informed me of the best items on the menu from his point of view, in Spanish. The young professor put me straight on a number of fine points, the tour replacement probably more fun than studying architecture again and asking a lot of irritating questions distracting administrators from their jobs.

So, what I'd recommend for my proposed project, right off the top, is the kind of spread-your-big-wings roofs I'd grown familiar with around the islands, maybe exaggerated slightly, for an esthetic and educational effect, rather than the formal academic look at the USFQ campus entrance building: ceremonial steps and tall columns included, if a little diminutive. You can see all that in the photo I'm including, one page back from here in this text. The columns look fine and can stay of course. The new structures I'm proposing would be to the left and mostly behind the building that is pictured there, page 66.

We'd be building up-slope to the north and east, providing new housing and a few classrooms, partially on artificial elevated rock substrate tamped down and topped by some real soil and planters in addition to the foundations for the new structures. Building on an elevated base, about ten feet higher than the existing buildings would provide safety except for the worst and rarest of tsunamis. The damage caused by the larger tsunamis would in any case be partially mitigated by simply being higher, less damage than for the existing infrastructure. In general, my guess is, looking around the Galápagos communities, the towns do not look that well prepared.

Another reason for building on an elevated platform: to help reverse global heating-related ocean rise. That's one of the major reasons for the whole ecocity project there, by way, hopefully, of effecting the design of cities

Ecotown addition to the Universidad San Francisco de Quito. This amounts to a small-scale college town in its own right. Most conspicuous are the numerous shade roofs and bridges connecting. Unseen are two narrow pedestrian streets making their way between buildings and also such systems as recycling, soil-building and bicycling into Puerto Baquerizo Moreno close by to the south, which is to the right of this drawing. The existing campus is in the lower right, the more faint part of the drawing.

everywhere. In itself, ecocity design and development is one of the most important things that can be done to slow and then even reverse global heating. That shouldn't be a surprise since cities are the largest creation of our species and their impacts massive and very damaging in their present form. In the chain of causes and effects, naturally, far less impact from cities taking hints from the Galápagos ecocity projects would mean less global heating and less sea level rise.

Just how far climate change and its effect on sea level will go before humans decide to apply a serious "full court press" to reverse the problem, no one knows. But a little artificial mound building, following the lead of cultures as distributed and ancient as the Middle Eastern Sumerians and Mississippi mound-building Native Americans, but in this present case near the coast, certainly can't hurt. I'll conclude this book with an idea for such an effort – that "full court press." I'll try describing where the ecocity and hence the Galápagos project would fit in such a strategy. Meantime we place this project on its modest artificial mound.

Most basically, the changes proposed here for an ecocity project amount to making the campus more like a real village with life's basic essentials, plus in this case higher education, all present and thriving. What's different than just that? The built facilities, if they work well, would be extremely light in their environmental impacts and with any luck would even build soils and quite consciously – and conscientiously according to the design intent – function like any other wild and natural complex living organism fitting beautifully into the ecological, even evolutionary, balances of its local and world environments. Then there is the message that should be able to be delivered broadly and outward to improve the future everywhere, should it function as designed and built.

And now, more details: The population and visitor flow there at the PBM new USFQ development project would probably be enough for only the dedicated residents who intentionally might want to buy very local, buy sundries, necessities, some school supplies, food, medicine, etc. in a minimalist "general store/drug store" and lunch snack place in addition to a school cafeteria if not already there, or create an expansion thereof.

But in addition to shaping the infrastructure, we'd target the student population to about double. With the schools growing renown, being a leading model project in how towns should be built, the point of the whole exercise in addition to the education within, expansion should be realistic, timed into a number of steps over a decade or two. The students could occasionally eat at the immediately next-door small restaurant or across the road on the beach side during the development time and in the "final" product.

If the micro drug store/general store with a few quick snacks is not quite up to the businesses next door and across the street on the beach side, with the iguanas and sea lions, there could be a coop for such things open a few hours two or three days a week. I've visited intentional communities of seventy or eighty people with such arrangements in my travels. Such limited shopping can work well and is often arranged partially to save money.

I'll feature two narrow pedestrian streets in the PBM project in which one "can get lost in the urban experience" and include a tiny movie theater. We will be looking at a set of buildings rising as high in a few places as five stories. There will be on the roof of the second floor, along with a couple big ceremonial native trees, a small plaza looking over the beach to the turquoise and azure sea, this plaza surrounded by two more stories of whatever "uses" were desired, say a coffee corner for late night coffee before tests and full moon or sliver crescent moon in twilight for your girlfriend or boyfriend and you during a marathon learning bout of "have to get this in before tomorrow's test" or "finish this paper by Thursday…"

The third floor, being on the elevated "keyhole plaza" level, would have some public uses like the café, plus bookstore, library, reading rooms, game room, lobby for some of the housing and for a small hotel for visitors… To be decided but with a splendid prospect view over the close-in trees, sand, rocks, sea, human and sea lion loungers, the café/sandwich shop across the street. Also seen: fishing boats bobbing gently between tourist boats here and there and more distant, the cargo ships headed into or out of the main PBM port. In the air lots of birds and none of them afraid of you, and the occasional airplanes bringing or taking away visitors, family, friends, teachers... This might sound a bit controversial, but I'd recommend removing a couple trees directly between the school and the beach as there is no view to the actual beach despite it being right there across the road and beyond the trees. The "notch view" of the beach would more or less double the effect of the view-surrounding architecture on the view-side of the third-floor keyhole plaza.

The fourth floor might be more housing, or conference meeting rooms, classrooms, whatever fine tuning would insert well in the overall scheme as it develops into the massing. And the roof of the fourth floor and fifth would be accessible, with outdoor furniture, planters and railings, waist high, probably glass, windscreen fences. Above that people-accessible roof, one or more of those strictly shade roofs overhead. Those would not have to cover everything. Some sunny spots would be up there too, some plants to attract the birds and be both colorful and why not educational tying in with the curriculum of Track # (1) Evolution, Ecology and Conservation. On all sides up there, we are surrounded by the whole island and sea wrap-around panorama. We are here about three stories higher than the second-floor deck you see in the photo of the existing main building entry.

One of my other favorite places in the world has, as a standard for almost all of its buildings, floating roofs, but of more sturdy construction than the Galápagos shade roofs. That's Bhutan and its ultimate roofs also spread out, often three or more feet over the walls of the building below, sometimes even wider than that. The edges of the roof structures there generally come down to only one or two vertical feet from the building walls and the outside, up-side roof of the top occupied floor. "Occupied" isn't quite the right word for what happens under that ultimate roof in Bhutanese architecture, on the flat

Above, part of a college village I proposed for an area of land called Anala in Bhutan near the border with India. Note the broad sheltering roofs, the bridges and free-standing glass elevator on the far right. A big honored tree is growing from a large tall planter. Smaller version of such planters are common in much of India, mostly in small plazas beside intersecting largely pedestrian streets.

surface under the floating roof, which experiences pretty much the outside temperature, moisture level and flow of the air around the whole structure.

Since all sorts of things are stored in the shelter of these highest roofs while precipitation and high-altitude sun is repelled, it is occupied by material items and air much more than by people. Under rain, snow and sun, the breeze slips through, but it is close to completely dry under this protection.

Those floating heavy construction roofs serve a somewhat different assignment than the Galápagos sun shade roofs but the comparison is interesting. Both protect. But, those upper roofs, generally with mildly sloping pitch in Bhutan can take some serious weather. What's needed for shade and the local wind loading that might be expected for the Galápagos is much lighter construction.

For the PBM project, don't forget vertical transportation. The roofs of the fourth floor puts people at the standing fifth, and the top accessible level is effectively at that level, but with no walls but waist level restraining ones, like the roof of the Charles Darwin Research Station over their café next door to Puerto Ayora. It is pretty far up on our new occupied rooftop so why not the second elevator for all the islands? There's only one now, on the western edge of Puerta Ayora at the Hotel Albatross mentioned or page 25. For our PBM project we will have just one elevator to add to the islands' inventory, a glass elevator that would be a delight to ride, and worth being considered an art piece – environmental art – in its own right. It would be a pleasure simply to move up and down, watching the landscape fall away as we go up, and rise toward us as we come down. The "art" could include etched glass local imagery below and above eye level as one stops at the various floors. One stop on the way would be at the small hotel lobby on the third floor or right next to its entrance doors. But most of the vertical access would be by those exterior shade-casting staircases.

Why not insert a building starting up-slope too, behind the existing campus buildings, and linked to our new structures with a bridge or two, tying the campus together three-dimensionally above ground level three or four stories up and even linking with existing buildings, maybe on a remodeled rooftop? For comparison, I've counted twenty buildings linked by ten bridges on the University of California campus in Berkeley. It's not that unusual on campuses already, a relatively un-sung virtue with some ecological points to make in supporting pedestrian access. For the PBM project these features are important for broadcasting the ideas embodied in the design – education – as a partial solution to some of our "access" (read "transport") problems everywhere.

With the post office a short walk away, if not possibly in the new structure, and other things missing in the overall campus, a bicycle ride to full small-town facilities in the town of Puerto Baquerizo Moreno itself, makes pretty much everything conveniently available.

Remembering the already indigenous and logical extra broad and shady roofs, why not something for the indigenous wildlife that seems minimally intimidated by people? Could we have plantings and shelter that the blue footed boobies might think charming enough to move into? Some other kind of bird? There may well be places created that attract native birds. The Ecosa Institute of Prescott, Arizona, for example, has plans to build a multi-story building with special features under the eaves to attract bats and swallows. Something similar for PBM I believe would be wonderful. Accumulating bird guano? Harvest it once in a while for garden fertilizer.

An addendum on recycling here, as suggested that the USFQ campus ecovillage project have soil building as one of its objectives. The islands have a problem with agriculture, which is lack of water and largely because the rocks that de Berlanga thought God sent down as stones from hell. Plus, the cracks in the cooling, hardening lava flows just suck whatever precipitation arrives downward into unavailability. Most vegetable foods are imported partially because farming is difficult due to this extremely poor "soil" situation, which is that there is almost none of it there. Several disastrous insects hitchhiked in on past food imports, which reinforces the other good reasons to improve farm production on the islands: keep as much local as possible.

But what if we used crushed rock and a very tough plastic or rubber-like sheet material to shunt the water that does precipitate to move it almost horizontally, slightly downslope through the soil instead of almost vertically down and away through cracks between rocks? The rolled out impermeable material, artificial soil on top, could do the job. Make peace with the petrol-chemical because it would probably be some sort of flexible sheet plastic. With the modest slope toward the sea that prevails there, the water would stay in the soil moving mainly horizontally and gently downward until transpired by plants, instead of seeping downward and out of availability. With the growing layer of soil on top, augmented steadily by organic decomposition of home, restaurant and farming waste the plastic would be protected from ultraviolet radiation by its covering of soil. Adding rock dust, which I noticed is produced in a steady small-stream quantity due to stone cutting adding up, why not steadily build more and more soil for intensive food production? I noticed a very large soccer field being flattened and compacted when I was there, with a crew rolling out a layer of sod. I also looked up machines for crushing stone on the Internet and there are lots of them. A long-term partial solution for improving food production on part of the 3% of the land available for such work should be possible.

11

Project in Puerto Ayora

The waterfront of Puerto Ayora is a mildly dynamic place, not quite buzzing with activity but rather kind of ambling along in small fishing town fashion… until a couple or few larger tourist boats arrive. Then it all gets rolling along, open for business. This place along Avenida Charles Darwin, is where most of the fish and the trapped lobsters become food and filter off to the restaurants and to some of the locals' homes. It's also the Islands main commercial area with bank as well as tourist orientation offices, tour companies' public presence, ticket sales kiosks for trips around the islands and ferries between and shops for the usual T-shirts, sun hats and ceramic mugs, small rubber bubbies and hammerhead shark toys and occasional calendars.

I couldn't find a single real book on the Galápagos Islands though, which surprised and disappointed me – I was looking for late night history, ecology or evolution reading. Out at the Charles Darwin Research Station there were only very few books for sale, too, and considering the amazing sights and animals and exotic plants to be seen there, I thought it a bit scandalous – or at least not very educational. On the positive side, there were a fair number of hotels with some introductory pamphlets as well as the standard tourist maps and relevant framed pictures and, in the less elegant hotels, sometimes posters with local wildlife and rather scientific explanations just tacked to the walls. Though I didn't take any professional tours, Sofia Darquea, the so

Above, this is the sunset view southeast from the Proinsular restaurant and café on the third floor of the Coop Grocery Store, at the west end of Avenida Charles Darwin, the main street of Puerto Ayora. Insular means "island" so the name means generally that the restaurant is a gift to, or for, the island. San Cristóbal Island is just beyond the horizon and a bit to the left of the center of this photo.

friendly, helpful and educational President of the Galápagos National Park Guides and Interpreters Association briefed me on the training the guides have to go through. The level of education dispensed on the front lines for the tourists looked like it had to be truly excellent. For the tours led by Stanford's William Durham, you should get serious credits toward some sort of a degree, he's so knowledgeable.

Of the many restaurants, a large proportion were elevated for views from the second floor or on the slightly elevated inland side of Avenida

From one of those restaurants, eating a fish dish again, appropriate to my now 650 miles out into the Pacific Ocean, I watched these enormous nasty black frigate birds with their forked tails and sharp angular swept back stingy narrow wings – *big* like giant bats – swirl in close overhead making the gulls and crows of Hitchcock's *The Birds* look passive and very small in comparison. I saw many a blue footed booby catch a big fish and be instantly pursued in a military-style dog fight with a frigate bird in pursuit until the harassed booby would drop the fish in mid-air and the attacker would swoop down underneath to catch the twice unfortunate fish while falling. A couple times it seemed the booby would intentionally fly low and drop the fish in a dense tangle of mangrove branches and into the stilt-walking roots that the frigate bird could never hope to penetrate as if to say, "OK, try to recover *this*, you jerk." Then the booby would just go casually back to dive-fishing afresh as if adding, "This is a snap."

Then there are the practical: hardware, drugstore, most basic clothing, and a good-sized clinic/small hospital, schools for the large proportion of children among the residents and open-air market, a couple sports fields, bait shops, church and a cemetery everything within a reasonably short walk or one dollar white taxi ride with pick-up box in back. A real small town, and being tourist-oriented, it is active into the night.

But as to my changes prescribed… Imagine the PBM suggestions but with rooftop accessibility at the sixth level, befitting a town of almost three times the population of PBM. A number of existing buildings already in Puerto Ayora are five stories, so to push up just a bit and not too far in making the point for three-dimensional development and its potential blessings shouldn't stretch acceptance by local people too far. One can get deep into the dynamics of ecocity design and layout in five or six stories: terrace and rooftop access, bridges between component buildings as at the Hotel Mainao, and the usually present broad shading roofs, canopies, overhangs and exterior stairs casting their cooling shadows. And remember this background information: the slow streets, a significant number of them one way and narrow, have significantly far more people moving about on bicycles, motor bikes (none I noticed excessively loud) and in those white cabs, and all were more numerous than private cars.

Being appropriately a project of about three times the size of the PBM project and on the main street, we have to also imagine that it would be built

Puerto Ayora ecocity project. We already have the basics down from our smaller PBM project. Now we just add more scale and detail.

over a couple decades as property would be accumulated by owners deciding they might want to build something eco-historic and hence another kind of draw and a good business investment. Their Municipal Planning Department of the Government of Puerto Ayora and Santa Cruz Island and the Galapagos National Park Directorate there in Puerto Ayora, could encourage that by helping to amend and expand the ecocity palate of regulations, especially local zoning.

Expect the same sort or features you are becoming familiar with in this book, but let's add here a couple more bridges between buildings linking terraces and roofs than featured at the PBM project and actually already built at the Hotel Mainao. Then we have more exterior staircases both curving and zig-zag. Also, two exterior glass elevators. And, not one but two or three pedestrian through-street hallways and a cozy very narrow alley or two providing the "lost in the urban" effect. These interior passageways, sometimes open to the sky or skylight, sometimes roofed-over, would also be provided with highly silvered "light tubes" that can bring serious light five stories down into buildings, and of course with some electric "area" lighting.

What else? A lot of mixed uses I won't reiterate at this point in our book. There is not one but three keyhole plazas, one looking out to sea, another obliquely angled to the usually clouded over top of the local mountain about eight miles inland and one with a view to mostly the town itself with a bit of landscape on the edge of that visual composition. Two of these mini-plazas are on terraces over the second floor, that is on the third-floor level and a third one on the fourth-floor level.

Finally, there's are two wrap-around view platforms on the roof of the sixth floor, one just a little higher than the other for esthetic variety, with their own sun sheltering roofs, like the Charles Darwin Research Station boasts and enjoys, but with a much more expansive view being considerably higher. That accessible roof of the CDRS Cafe, by the way, does have good views all around but I couldn't help wishing it was just one story higher to see much better over the low-rising native trees and cactuses that block almost all the view to the edge of land with the Pacific.

Let's have two glass, elevators, one looking inland at the city and central island mountain, and the other obliquely out across Avenue Charles Darwin at an angle to Academy Bay. And there would be at this scale room for three or four interior pedestrian streets and even a closed mini-plaza with swirl around interior balcony punctuated by a couple curving staircases. Skylights galore.

12

The ecotropolis mapping system
pulls it all together

…and guides us into a healthier future. I featured this tool for transforming our villages, towns and cities back on page 51. Considering how important this overall literal map for change can be, though, I'll go into a little more detail here near the closing of this book.

Most fundamentally this set of maps and related ideas shows us what is most needed for moving away from two-dimensional scatterization of our community infrastructures toward "centers-oriented development" in the functionally diverse and pedestrian-first mode. I advocate for what I call "the transportation hierarchy" which states: "feet first, then pedestrian bridges, stairs and elevators, then bicycles, then rail transport, then busses, and lastly, cars" with that last one – automobiles – actively discouraged, except for those living in genuine rural circumstances.

The ecotropolis mapping system is indispensable conceptually whether worked up in actual map form or just described. However, actually making and using such a map is head and shoulders over just thinking and talking about it. Mapping forces specificity and is probably just plain crucial to making progress toward cities that actually play a healthy role on the planet – like any other complex living organism, for which it can be a highly educational analogy. As Huey Johnson, Resources Secretary for the State of California in Jerry Brown's first two terms as Governor back in the 1970s and 1980s liked to say, "No map, no meeting." He was also founder of Trust for Public Land and if no maps, how to establish and run land trusts for preserving natural environments, bringing healthy open spaces like parks, gardens and playgrounds to cities or any other thing TPL accomplished? This might be said in regard to ecotropolis thinking, "No map, difficult to imagine getting an ecocity project conceived, then built, much less promulgate such built communities around the world."

There is a problem immediately recognizable, however, when you withdraw the map from your travel tube, and spread it out on a table, even for most of your environmentalist friends. You can see their eyes roaming about getting orient for a couple seconds. Then, zeroing in on their houses' locations they say, "Wow, why would want to demolish my house and bring back an orchard, row crops or a bunch of cattle and coyotes?" If their house is close to a designated center where development would be encouraged or if part of such an up-zoned center, the panic gets worse... "You'd allow a six-story apartment on my block?!!!"

But who said the difficult things would be easy? Are you serious about facing the challenges of our times or not? First of all, these changes take time and many opportunities for thinking them through. With good design and public process they would also be pleasurable, convenient and be profitable for those thinking it all through and invested in carefully. Slow down and consider the alternatives – like the disasters of climate change on the one hand, or that incremental steps in the right direction actually providing a far more interesting and varied environment with addition of more open spaces close to human activity. What if, for example four or five houses on your block were removed and a public park or community garden were there instead, or some new commercial farming. What if in the opposite direction in ecocity design a couple blocks away you now had more pedestrian-friendly places to shop, eat, gather with friends, and with great views? Not so bad and if slow, dedicated and steady changes in such direction were on-going, life would be getting more varied and healthy all the time.

About the disaster we should definitely avoid there's a telling comment by the elegant wordsmith and author, mainly on food and agriculture, if comment in the broadest strokes of history and with trenchant philosophical wanderings, in his many books. That's Michael Pollan and he makes this comment in someone else's book, in Paul Hawken's *Drawdown*.

Pollan says in a section of the book entitled "Why Bother?" (bother drawing down carbon from the atmosphere and sequestering it into the soils of the Earth), "...for me the most upsetting moment in [the movie] *An Inconvenient Truth* came long after Al Gore scared the hell out of me constructing an utterly convincing case that the very survival of life on Earth as we know it is threatened by climate change. No, the really dark moment came during the closing credits when we are asked to... change our light bulbs. That's when it got really depressing. The vast disproportion between the magnitude of the problem Gore had described and the puniness of what he was asking us to do about it was enough to sink your heart."

Are we really serious when we call for strong medicine to cure our largest problems? If we honestly want them solved it will take some very well thought out and conscientious work on the part of great numbers of us. And coming up with a far lighter footprint for city, town and village than we have at present is a very large slice of what's needed. I'm sure far, far too many people would take one look at the idea of major urban design change, including a map being very specific about it, and say, "Well, let's talk some

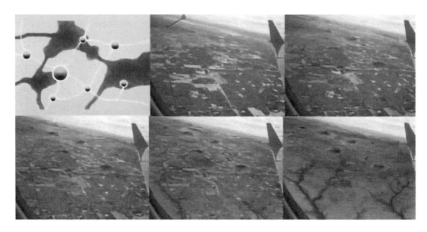

Above, long term transition from thin and scattered megalopolis to ecotropolis is illustrated, top far left, by some abstracted 2-D sprawl – dark gray areas – and dots of three sizes suggesting more compact roughly circular but 3-D development. The other five images start with a photo I took flying over Denver, Colorado in winter snow, its downtown at the point of the red "hat pin" barely visible, and its vast car dependent suburbs spread over tens of thousands of acres. Expect at least a century for such a transition, but as time moves on, all systems go lighter and lighter on destructive land and life impacts.

more about changing that light bulb. Let's go looking for it...(then I won't have to do much after all)."

Current car/sprawl city is, if one be honest about it, obviously land-, energy-, material-, money- and time-squandering, demanding far too much of the planet's surface, resources and peoples' patience in traffic jams. Meantime this mapping system helps make it possible for cities to become as healthy as normal complex living organisms. Natural plants and animals have waste products that are decomposed and recycled into the biosphere with other organisms picking up the tasks along the way. It's known they can do this and *we*, us humans, can do this too. It's one of the few real slam dunks out there. Built environments could help greatly through everyday operations, sending almost all such resources back into soil enrichment or by assiduous recycling making material things of future use to us humans... and the rest of the biosphere… if we design them right. In this, on the city and regional scale, ecotropolis maps are key.

So once we decide on the locations of the centers, the downtowns can become ecocities, major district centers can become ecotowns and neighborhood center can become ecovillages. While the land recovers from asphalt, concrete and monoculture lawns, it can become newly restored natural habitats and agricultural environments, restored waterways and shorelines and special places like ridgelines with stunning views, notable rock outcrops and magnificent grass, brush, forest, desert and on and on landscapes.

And the role of ecocity projects in all this such as ones we might imagine on the Galápagos Islands? Waking us up to the basic principles involved and steps we could take to solve a very large slice of our great and most intractable problems becomes a real possibility.

13

Placing Yourself in Arcosanti and Fire-safe Village

Before we conclude this book, I have two more images I want to share. First, a modified version of Arcosanti, Arizona, then second, a fire-safe village to re-suggest the versatility of ecocity thinking and its range of solutions offered, whether from the Galápagos or anywhere, for "Change can happen at the speed of thought".

I lived for a year at Paolo Soleri's experimental town of Arcosanti, Arizona, the last half of 1976 and first half of 1977. I was even one of the 20 alert and lucky people present on the first day of actual construction too, which was in 1970. My experience there was a deep emersion in ideas about city designs and ambitions to improve them. I found the experience a real delight but had some criticisms. For example, though the idea behind the effort to build this town was to embody a more three-dimensional model for the future of cities, rendering them actually healthy for the planet, the buildings on site there were in fact strung out from west to east along the edge of a mildly dramatic mesa, one of those flat-topped big hills or small mountains so common in the US Southwest. From across the valley on the south side, looking north, the view to the busily building Arcosanti was quite striking, potentially inspiring. How to make the most of it?

There is a steep slope on that mesa's south side and the tallest building, at the equivalent of six stories for most buildings, though one floor there is something more than three typical stories high. The building is called Crafts III (or Crafts 3) and the largest space there is an open space for meals, meetings and display of models and drawings. It features a magnificent view through three enormous circular windows nearly floor to very high ceiling, with doors in the middle of the circles. These great round windows face east, south and west. Crafts III is constructed on the downward slope of the mesa rising to only a few feet above the top of the mesa. It had always surprised me a bit that to enhance the three-dimensional message of the effort of building Arcosanti, considering the photos to come from that looking-north perspective across the small valley to the south, that instead of building off to the east along the lip of the mesa in a basically linear arrangement, which has been done, another building of about the same height should be placed behind the "downward" situated building, Crafts III. The new building would be on the top of the mesa, back from the edge but close to the edge and to Crafts III.

The result would be a view from the south northward toward the occupied structures, together rising eleven or twelve visual stories, though you'd only need the engineering to support six stories. We could also feather a spectacular twelve story exterior glass elevator there with short bridges to both buildings. My comments on the subject however were not considered that important. Or maybe I didn't articulate them that well at the time. But I remain convinced that a good opportunity was lost, and I was there from the first day of construction in 1970 and believe, with knowing Paolo for five years by then, I should have been taken more seriously.

But what, with this thinking is not built now, *can nonetheless be drawn.* What I come up with follows now: an arrangement I thought would sell the idea behind Arcosanti far better to the public than what is actually there, which by the way has stalled out. That is, there has been no serious large-scale construction in the last 25 years. What it could have been… Well, maybe it will experience a Renaissance somehow, but meantime I think there are lessons there for thinking through what an ecocity project in the Galápagos could deliver, and the drawing I'm about to show you might help inform better more human and "ecological" towns into the future.

Something of a side note but a bit of an historical explanation for why my ideas were not taken seriously in the first few years of construction at Arcosanti, say 1970 through 1975: Soleri admitted that to build a community for the projected six or seven thousand people he had in mind was a long way farther down the road than he would be able to motivate in the first, say, decade of building there. He put forward in drawings of versions of his vision of a complete structure but never worked out an incremental set of growing stages from the small scale which by around 1975 housed three or four dozen people, to an eventual project of enormous investment. He pointed out as honestly as he could imagine that people would need to see his vision as crucially important and invest in it far more than would be expected in the first ten years. The problem was that people in any serious numbers or with enough power to make the leap to the eventual built-out ecotown by writing legally binding policy and/or donating serious money simply did not materialize to support the eventual goal. I remained convinced that expressions of the three-dimensional model was extremely important, in terms Soleri often used himself, calling the effort "indispensable." Few agreed with him, or with me for that matter.

So, I drew up what I thought did two things: represent in a set of drawings – one of these I'm including here below – a representation of a genuinely three-dimensional model. Secondly, I hope to drag you into my mind set while drawing such imagery, because I put myself into the environment pictured, that I have drawn, and believe it to be a truly inspiring place to be. If I can convince people viewing the drawing that it would be an extremely pleasurable place, I've made some progress. The scheme then is to take what was there and built around 1975 and, through the drawing, bridge over to getting three-dimensional enough that people can begin to "get it," looking across the small valley from the south toward the structure in the north, so that we can all imagine ourselves being in such a structure and very actively enjoying it.

We'd have plants, birds and insects at our shoulders. We'd be having a cup of coffee or tea, maybe a late afternoon quitting-time beer, on, say the

Above, a once-that-could-have-been stage in the construction of Arcosanti, Arizona designed to illustrated three-dimensional structuring of a small town developing and utilizing some of the design ideas and detailing some of architect Paolo Soleri's ideas and style, forms and colors.

twelfth-floor terrace and just down the elevator and "out the door" the local natural environment. Then we could clearly understand the non-disruptive nature of such an ecotown, leaving its immediate surroundings, whether natural or agricultural, in sound healthy condition.

I imagine the small within the large. This applies down to the size of the projects I'm proposing in this book for the Galápagos as about the smallest size at which we can exercise these ecocity basic thoughts and arrangements that are at the same time large enough to make the essential points and communicate the full potential of the mode of design and the very excellent and healthy outcomes to be expected from application of such modes.

Try placing yourself in the drawing. You've arrived among the fall colors of the trees on your level seven stories over the mesa top and 13 over the base of the Crafts III building, the building looking rather square in the lower left of the drawing. You are near the base of the yellow and orange tree in its fall colors, toward the left of center in the illustration. A crane is working away, completing a building. You are looking south toward our position for the drawing looking north.

Off to your left, if you are near the yellow/orange fall colors, and behind you are two bridges linking taller buildings, about six stories taller than where you are sitting. Several of the terraces on the way up are publicly accessible. You've just enjoyed a mildly breath-taking ride up one of the exterior glass elevators. From where you are you can see, as I did from the real Arcosanti's café in Craft III back in 1975, a coyote on the ground to the south and a couple circling hawks, though being a few stories higher, the coyote you see now looks a little smaller, farther away, while the hawks are much closer and look larger. It's urban enough you might even have a few pigeons.

Imagine the elevated experience surrounded by views out to the landscape around, with desert plants but few human artifacts surrounding, attracting the likes of, not to sound too cliché about it, but attracting birds, butterflies and bees in those elevated, but solidly grounded places in the air. Being Arizona, you might even have a few turquoise striped lizards darting around the rooftop and terrace cactuses and bushes and doing their usual push-ups. Here you are connected to the igneous stone below with steel impregnated concrete walls, columns and cross-bracing. Within a 30 second walk, you're crossing a dramatic arched bridge with the rich colors of Soleri's concrete structures, in bold patterns in view. Housing is all around, too, office space nearby, drafting rooms, and up at the tourist and guest reception rooms at the highest level of the complex, you're able to purchase all the information you could hope for in illustrating and explaining what Arcosanti and its fundamental ideas are all about. Including this by then pretty old and dated book.

I imagine relaxing up there as people do now simply sitting on top of the tallest existing structures there watching the sunsets and roaming thunder storms dragging their columns of dark gray rain, blue-purple lightning bolts and brilliant rainbows about the landscape in Arcosanti's dry prickly environs. But in the version you see here you are three times as high as the early Crafts III building facing a sometimes truly extravagantly beautiful view surrounded by the humanly familiar at your feet and solid down to the concrete foundation on hard stone lava – exactly like building on lava in the Galápagos

Islands.

The distant and the close-in are here harmonized. The natural, the human. The message: not so hard to build if we decide to and it can maybe even participate fully in healthy evolution here on planet Earth.

One last case of assembled specifics before saying good-bye to *The Galápgos Islands: Evolution's Lessons for Cities of the Future*: fire-safe village.

It isn't easy convincing people there are better ways of building and living. The fire that destroyed Paradise, California dramatized the problem. It erupted on a hot, dry, windy morning November 8 of 2018 and burned for 17 days, destroying 18,804 structures killing at least 86 people, probably 88 with two unaccounted for ever since, while destroying the entire town that had housed 30,000 residents. The whole community turned to ashes, probably including the two people who apparently disappeared entirely.

There is a fire-safe ecocity solution that I learned after the 1991 Oakland Hills Firestorm, the worst loss of housing and lives in the state's fire history to that time. It destroyed 3,375 homes, killing 25, small compared to the Paradise conflagration. After that catastrophe I attended many of the community recovery meetings in Oakland and Berkeley at which the local fire departments praised the strategy of using swimming pools and gasoline powered water pumps and large hoses to fight fires.

Compact development, a swimming pool or two, pumps and hoses and you have an ecocity solution to living in rural areas in security – if you can stand apartment living in rich social and commercial circumstances surrounded by practically totally natural environment.

Adding the compact and true community design, with apartments of not even large scale, say five story on average, narrow streets and all, highly mixed use, basically a European layout without even going to more advanced ecocity features and placing a community swimming pool or two in the direction almost all fires come from in fire country, and we are well on our way. Add a wide fire break in the vegetation around those few blocks of structures, and we'd be replacing around 100 acres of typical thinly scattered single-family houses, a pattern not very different from Paradise's prior to their fire. As in my illustration here, with five or so water pumps and hoses creating a "curtain of water," as the fire departments advised, against the advancing flames, and you'd be safe, with just a little courage to be there defending. With one or two pumps and hoses putting out spot fires created by sparks and firebrands caught in the updrafts and hurled forward of the fire front, such a community would be defended easily by a concentration of fire fighters much smaller in number than called out to try to suppress fires covering many dozens of times the land area of the compact village. Words direct from the fire fighters: you only have to defend your property for about twenty minutes or half an hour and the major impact of the fire front has moved on or died down. This kind of defense is much easier and far less costly than mounting a defense for 25 to many more times the land area in scattered development similar to the pattern in Paradise in 2018 before the fire, and in Oakland too for that matter in 1991.

14

The media that delivers the news – and the news itself

The message has to get out: cities can be reshaped to contribute generously to solving climate change, species extinctions, and many other problems while creating graceful and rewarding, socially and ecologically enriching built communities. The Galápagos Islands provide a thoroughly unique location from which this message can be effectively broadcast, providing for that message those powerful lessons of evolution evident there.

And remember that line from the Greenpeace activist I like so much: "Change can happen at the speed of thought".

And there is nothing so powerful among communications media, as physical models and real physical activity enlivening such models from construction of them to daily life within. It's called walking the talk when it gets down to physical manifestations, and creating the environment for the walk, helping the walk be relevant, meaningful, effective. Walk, don't drive!

One last point here I'd like to make. Sure, ecocity solutions are crucially important, but I'm not saying it's the only very important thing to be doing and building. There are about six things utterly indispensable for a thriving survival into the deep future that need our focused laser-like attention. That's not too much to keep in mind all at one time. By now we've figured out general conservation, recycling and "cleaning up" our world for fresh air, clean water and soil. That's the slam dunk part. But I want to emphasize in closing, that we need also to deal with our vast numbers – overpopulation.

We need to get to a far healthier agriculture system more in tune with the organic and seasonal. We need to realize the importance of taking carbon out of the air and sequestering it into soils, the point of Paul Hawken's book *Drawdown*, as well as understanding the necessity for building eco-communities from village to city scale as represented in this book.

Then there are two big issues not so physical but mental, psychological, spiritual: the first of those being generosity, giving back to the Earth that so generously supports us and not being so materialistic and greedy. Then lastly there's education… about all the above, as if healthy evolution itself depends on us now, as in fact it does. None of those Big Ones is easy to accomplish. But if we don't have long strides toward solving those linked Big Ones, we can expect magnifying enormously the problems we already have.

But put all those pieces together and see how they relate to one another and we have one of those famous "whole systems" views that can be so helpful. This is the "full court press," a term from basketball of all things, so popular in the US, richest country in the world and in China, our most populous country. As so many in these two places love basketball, we need an even greater love of that small number of indispensable moves toward a better future of which getting cities right is one of the absolute essentials, the ultimate full court press in which the whole team is tuned up, alert, coordinated and in best of form.

Now I leave it up to you. Earth Day 2020 is coming in a few months, if for most of you readers it will be in the past already by the time you see this small book. It will almost certainly be the largest event shared by people on this planet to that date, likely to be around two billion people. Will many people be considering ecocity design for future cities at that time? What *will* our cities be like in our future, our children's future? The towns and the villages? Will our built environments still be bad citizens to the rest of our fellow passengers on planet Earth even to the climate system that envelops and nurtures us all in space and time? What *can* we learn from evolution after all?

The good news is that the power is in our hands… if the idea can get into our heads.

Acknowledgements

This short book was suggested to me by Ron Chilcote of the Foundation for Sustainability and Innovation. His kind thought came through in the shadow of the failure of my work for an international conference on evolution and cities in early December 2019, conceived for location on the legendary – and for good reason legendary – Galápagos Islands. Maybe a major conference there later, a great idea in any case but just not in time this time for Earth Day 2020.

Hopefully, this book amounts to a way to broadcast out from those Enchanted Isles some of the content I'd imagined we'd be dealing with there. Perhaps a few new ideas forged in those lands of once-flaming lava erupting under the equatorial sun, up through the Antarctic's cold Humboldt Current, will be broadcast out around the world… from this book at least. I had some new ideas there on the Enchanteds, augmented by some notions discussed with Darren Sears and Sofia Darquea during my two visits. Plus, Mr. Chilcote's foundation made a helpful grant to encourage me along the way.

I wrote this book without much help, unlike some of my books, being a short book, except for Stacy Becker's help. She's my friend in Arcata who has contributed proofing and some editing with the last two of my much longer books and been discussing ideas with me for this book – very helpful with this work too. So, a very friendly thanks to all four of you, Ron, Darren, Sofia and Stacy.

The spark of the idea to bring the guidance of evolution for cities to the Galápagos hit me like a lightning bolt. I remember that split second. I said to myself, "Oh my God! This make sense. I have to be there. I have to do this." Those four short sentences shot through my mind faster than a single normal word. There wasn't the slightest hesitation. Thanks Rosalia Arteaga Serrano for brining me to that slice of the instantly disappearing present becoming an all-consuming conclusion driving me onward. Jose Merlo, by coincidence, your exposition on your agriculture experiments you were describing at Rosalia's breakfast, exactly then… thank you and the Fates and the Sirens of the Endless World Ocean. So I cashed in my savings and went – hello Galápagos, hello better future.

And it's a real pleasure giving credit to the folks whose great works have been such important ideas herein. Thank you, Mr. Charles Darwin, and Paolo Soleri, and Lynn Margulis. They would believe, as do I and I trust you readers will also, that – ironically – only us humans can save us now… from ourselves.

If all goes well, this book will help.

Bibliography

Architecture Without Architects, Bernard Rudolfsky, Doubleday & Company, Inc., Garden City, New York, 1964

Autokind vs. Humankind – an Analysis of Tyranny, a Proposal for Rebellion, a Plan for Reconstruction, Kenneth Schneider, Schoken Books, New York, 1972

Biophilic Cities – Integrating Nature into Urban Design and Planning, Timothy Beatley, Island Press, Washington, DC, 2011

Building a Win-Win World – Life Beyond Global Economic Warfare, Hazel Henderson, Berrett-Koehler Publishers, San Francisco, 1996
Green Urbanism – Learning from European Cities, Timothy Beatley, Island Press, Washington, DC, 2000

Cooked – a Natural History of Transformation, Michale Pollan, Penguin Press, New York, 2014

Carl Sagan – A Life, Keay Davidson, John Wiley & Sons, Inc., New York, 1999

Coevolution – Genes, Culture and Human Diversity, William Durham, Stanford University Press, Stanford, California, 2001

Darwin – the Life of a Tormented Evolutionist, Adrian Desmond & James Moore, Warner Books, New York, 1991

Darwin's Ghosts – the Secret History of Evolution, Rebecca Stott, Random House, New York, 2012

The Future of Life, Edward O. Wilson, Alfred A. Knopf, New York, 2002

To Govern Evolution – Further Adventures of the Political Animal, Walt Anderson, Harcourt Brace Jovanovich Publishers, Boston, San Diego, New Yok, 1987

The Great Transition – Shifting from Fossil Fuels to Solar and Wind Energy, Lester Brown, W. W. Norton, New York, 2015

High Tide on Main Street – Rising Sea Level and the Coming Coastal Crisis, John

Englander, the Science Bookshelf, Boca Raton, Florida, 2012

Invisible Cities, Italo Calvino, Harvest Books, Harcourt Brace and Company, New York, 1972

The Language of Cities, Deyan Sdjic, Penguin Books, Milton Keynes, 2017

A Place of Power – the American Episode in Human Evolution, Walt Anderson, Goodyear Publishing, Santa Monica, California, 1976

The Preindustrial City Past and Present, Gideon Sjoberg,
Saved by Development – Preserving Environmental Areas, Farmland and Historic Landmarks with transfer of Development Rights, Rick Pruetz, AICP, Arje Press, Burbank, California, 1997

Resilient Cities – Responding to Peak Oil and Climate Change, Peter Newman, Timothy Beatley, and Heather Boyer, Island Press, Washington, DC, 2009

Saving the Planet – How to Shape an Environmentally Sustainable Global Economy – Lester Brown, Christopher Flavin, Sandra Postel, W. W. Norton & Company, New York, London, 1991

Streetcar Suburbs – The Process of Growth in Boston 1870-1900, Sam B. Warner, Jr., Harvard University Press and Anthium, Boston, 1962

Transforming Cities with Transit – Transit and Land-use Integration for Sustainable Urban Development, Hiroaki Siziuki, Robert Cervo, and Kanako Luchi, World Bank, 2013

Unnatural Selection – How We Are Changing Life, Gene by Gene, Emily Monosson, Island Press, Washington, DC, 2015

The World Without Us, Alan Weisman, Thomas Dunne Books, St. Martin's Griffin, New York, 2007

Index

Random thought along the way
to think more about...

"Never give up!"

OK, so I gave up the conference, but I'll never give up the idea – the real on the Galápagos + evolution's lesson for cities = vast progress for human relations with nature: "Peace on Earth, Peace *with* Earth." Because I know, though flesh and blood be temporary, ideas are forever, and even if forgotten, if based on principles true to the physics and geometry of the real, those good ideas can come back to live forever in this universe just as can any of the elements, the existence and dynamics of solar systems, the secrets of the universe becoming ever better known, the geology of hot planet cores moving within, the way water makes so many things possible...

Made in the USA
Middletown, DE
22 March 2020